FUN IS FUN AND DONE IS DONE

FUN IS FUN AND DONE IS DONE

Stephen King Connections and Easter Eggs

Michael Roch

ISBN-13: 979–8–9861521–1–0 (hardback)
ISBN-13: 979–8–9861521–0–3 (paperback)
ISBN-13: 979–8–9861521–2–7 (ebook)

Fun is fun and done is done.

—Jean Parker, “Riding the Bullet”

Fun is fun and done is done.

—Owen Underhill, *Dreamcatcher*

Fun is fun and done is done.

—Susannah Dean, *The Dark Tower*

Contents

Introduction

When reading Stephen King, Constant Readers often experience déjà vu and see that many of his works are intertwined. We return to familiar fictional towns, learn more about favorite characters, and see other elements again and again. These towns, characters, etc. provide strong connections among his stories. Other times, we come upon Easter Eggs—familiar themes or references that don't directly connect any works but remind us of something we'd seen before.

There are countless wacky connection ideas out there; none are given here. Many of those fall under the Blue Berry Syndrome. We know blueberries are safe to eat. Good and sweet, they make wonderful additions to cereal and muffins. But, it's not a good idea to eat just any old blue berry you find in the woods; it could be poisonous. As Alex Reiger explained to Reverend Jim in "The Call of the Mild" episode on *Taxi*, "While all blueberries are blue, not all blue berries are blueberries."

One such connection is that Carrie, because she was telekinetic, was a Breaker. That's the Blue Berry Syndrome. While the group of Breakers includes telekinetics, not all telekinetics are Breakers.

Another example tries to connect "The Mist" with *Firestarter* by saying the Arrowhead Project was run by the Shop. While there's no doubt the Arrowhead Project was a clandestine government operation, not all clandestine government operations are run by the Shop.

Connections and Easter Eggs have a blue berry relationship as well. While all connections are Easter Eggs, not all Easter Eggs are connections. In this book, the book's title is underlined for connections, while **[Easter Egg]** precedes the non-underlined title for Easter Eggs that I feel aren't strong enough to be actual connections.

Closely Related Combinations

The following short story and eight volumes are so closely related, this book refers to them collectively as *The Dark Tower*:

"The Little Sisters of Eluria"
I: *The Gunslinger*
II: *The Drawing of the Three*
III: *The Waste Lands*
IV: *Wizard and Glass*
IV.V: *The Wind Through the Keyhole*
V: *Wolves of the Calla*
VI: *Song of Susannah*
VII: *The Dark Tower*

When "The Little Sisters of Eluria" was first published in *Legends: Short Novels by the Masters of Modern Fantasy*, the Table of Contents identified it as "The Dark Tower: The Little Sisters of Eluria."

Similarly, while *Hearts in Atlantis* contains five stories, they are so closely related, we can refer to them collectively as if they make up a novel.

Warning

Spoilers in this book are like roaches in *Creepshow*'s "They're Creeping Up on You"—they're everywhere.

Locale Connections

Stephen King's fictional towns provide the favorite form of connection.

Arcadia Beach, NH

The Talisman: Jack Sawyer started his travels from Arcadia Beach.

The Tommyknockers: After a week-long drunken blackout, Gard woke up on Arcadia Beach and talked with Jack.

Arnette, TX

The Stand: Stu Redman and others were from Arnette. Stu was the only known survivor.

"The Monkey": Hal Shelburn and his family lived in Arnette.

The Tommyknockers: Maine State Police Trooper Claudell Weems pulled in radio broadcasts from Medford, MA; Friday, ND; and Arnette, TX.

Desperation: Steve Ames's Aunt Betty was from Arnette.

11/22/63: The Denholm Lions beat the Arnette Bears.

Castle Rock, ME

I consider myself Stephen King's Number One Fan—you other Number One Fans probably disagree!—and I consider Castle Rock to be his Number One Town as it is the scene of action in many novels and stories and mentioned in several others. Derry is a close runner-up, but after recounting the votes, Castle Rock still wins.

The Stand: After Randall Flagg was defeated, Fran Goldsmith wanted to go to western Maine, perhaps Castle Rock.

The Dead Zone: Thanks to Frank Dodd, *The Dead Zone* is our first good look at Castle Rock.

Cujo: Terror struck Castle Rock again, this time from a rabid dog.

"The Lonesome Death of Jordy Verrill": 1) Jordy's farm was five miles from Castle Rock. 2) The office of Dr. Peter V. Higgins was in Castle Rock.

"Rita Hayworth and Shawshank Redemption": Red was from Castle Rock.

"The Body": Chris Chambers, Teddy Duchamp, Gordon Lachance, and Vern Tessio trekked from Castle Rock to South Harlow to find Ray Brower's body.

"Stud City": Johnny May's Dodge would run fast on the road from Gates Falls to Castle Rock.

"Mrs. Todd's Shortcut": The Todds had a summer home on Castle Lake in Castle Rock.

"Nona": The Hollises lived in Harlow, across the river from Castle Rock. The story started at Joe's Good Eats in Augusta, ME, and ended in a Castle Rock cemetery.

"Uncle Otto's Truck": Uncle Otto lived in Castle Rock.

"Gramma": The Bruckners lived in Castle Rock.

IT: Beverly Rogan remarked about the crazy Castle Rock cop who killed women.

The Dark Half: The Beaumonts had a summer home in Castle Rock.

"The Sun Dog": This story introduced us to Ace Merrill's uncle, Pop Merrill.

Needful Things: Leland Gaunt had such fun setting Castle Rock residents against one another.

Gerald's Game: Sheriff Ridgewick of Castle Rock caught cemetery aficionado Raymond Andrew Joubert.

"It Grows on You": Joe Newall's house grew in Castle Rock.

Bag of Bones: Castle Rock was one of TR-90's nearest towns. It now has a hospital.

The Girl Who Loved Tom Gordon: 1) Trisha McFarland listened to Red Sox games on WCAS, a Castle Rock station. 2) Castle Rock now has a Castle Rock Speedway and a Maine State Police barracks.

Dreamcatcher: Castle Rock's WCAS reported winter storms.

"The Man in the Black Suit": Castle Stream forked in Motton. One branch flowed to Kashwakamak Township, the other to Castle Rock.

"Riding the Bullet": An old man gave the hitchhiking Alan Parker a ride through several Maine towns, including Castle Rock.

Lisey's Story: Lisey and Scott Landon lived in Castle Rock.

Blaze: Gerald Clutterbuck Realty of Castle Rock listed the old Hetton House property for sale or lease.

"N.": N. lived on the View in Castle Rock.

Under the Dome: Castle Rock bordered Chester's Mill to the southwest.

"A Good Marriage": Bob Anderson took Darcy Madsen to a Saturday street sale in Castle Rock.

11/22/63: Castle Rock was near Lisbon Falls.

Doctor Sleep: Dr. John Dalton's rounds included Castle Rock.

Revival: Castle Rock was down Route 9 from Harlow.

"Premium Harmony": Mary and Ray Burkett lived in Castle Rock.

"Squad D": Josh Bortman, the only surviving member of Squad D, was from Castle Rock.

Gwendy's Button Box: Gwendy Peterson grew up in Castle Rock.

Elevation: Scott Carey continuously lost weight (but kept his mass) in Castle Rock.

Gwendy's Magic Feather: Gwendy Peterson grew up in Castle Rock and later lived on Castle View.

"Mr. Harrigan's Phone": Each time Craig's father was selected as Salesman of the Month, he'd treat Craig to dinner at Marcel's in Castle Rock.

Gwendy's Final Task: Sheila Brigham retired and moved from Castle Rock to Florida.

Chamberlain, ME

Carrie: Chamberlain, ME, is best known as the setting for *Carrie*.

'Salem's Lot: Ben Mears drove north on the Maine turnpike to return to Jerusalem's Lot after a long absence. Had he missed the exit, he would've come upon Chamberlain then Lewiston.

"The Body": Ray Brower lived in Chamberlain, about forty miles from Castle Rock.

"It Grows on You": Singer "Country" Ken Corriveau retired from music and moved from Castle Rock to Chamberlain.

Gerald's Game: Because of a fire in Castle Rock a year before, Sheriff Ridgewick sent most detainees to Chamberlain and Norway. Raymond Andrew Joubert, who desecrated corpses in cemeteries throughout western Maine and scared the crap out of Jessie Burlingame, was one such detainee.

Chester's Mill, ME

"N.": Amateur photographer N. took pictures in Chester's Mill and other towns along the Androscoggin River.

Under the Dome: One day, a transparent alien dome encapsulated Chester's Mill.

"Drunken Fireworks": For the last Fourth of July Arms race, cars lined roads toward TR–90 and Chester's Mill.

Cleaves Mills, ME

The Dead Zone: Rookie Cleaves Mills High School teachers Sarah Bracknell and Johnny Smith met while chaperoning a freshman dance.

The Tommyknockers: 1) Bobbi Anderson moved from Cleaves Mills to Haven when she inherited Uncle Frank's place. 2) Andy Torgeson and Claudell Weems were state troopers from the Cleaves Mills barracks. 3) Johnny Smith had taught in Cleaves Mills.

"Weeds": 1) Jordy Verrill lived in Cleaves Mills—but it was in New Hampshire! "The Lonesome Death of Jordy Verrill" moved his farm to Maine. 2) Dr. Condon and Doc Oakley each had an office in Cleaves Mills.

IT: People from Cleaves Mills and other nearby towns partied at The Black Spot.

Lisey's Story: Lisey had an apartment in Cleaves Mills while a part-time student at UMO. Her wedding reception was held at The Rock in Cleaves Mills.

Gwendy's Button Box: The rape-murder of a Cleaves Mills girl didn't quite fit the rape M.O. of Frankie Stone.

Dark Score Lake in Maine

Dark Score Lake is in the lakes district of western Maine. The Foreword to the ebook of *Dolores Claiborne* says it is in Sharbot, ME. Sharbot is mentioned nowhere else.

Gerald's Game: As Jessie Mahout sat on her father's lap to watch the eclipse from their Dark Score Lake summer home, . . .

Dolores Claiborne: Dark Score Lake appears on the map showing the totality of the eclipse across Maine.

Bag of Bones: The Noonans had a summer home on Dark Score Lake.

Lisey's Story: Naresh Patel, of Patel's Market in Castle View, wore a Dark Score Lake T-shirt.

Gwendy's Button Box: Lucas Browne's family had a summer cabin on Dark Score Lake.

Gwendy's Final Task: Norris Ridgewick enjoyed fishing here.

The Dark Tower (the Tower)

The Dark Tower: Roland Deschain sought the Dark Tower. The Crimson King sought to destroy it.

Black House: Parkus explained that Jack Sawyer's mission was to keep the Crimson King from using Tyler Marshall as a Breaker to cause the Dark Tower to fall.

"Ur": Wesley Smith violated the Paradox Laws and caused the Tower to tremble.

Gwendy's Final Task: The taheen sought Gwendy's button box to destroy the Tower.

Delain

The Eyes of the Dragon: King Roland ruled Delain.

The Dark Tower: Walter Padick was born a farmer's boy in Delain. He grew up to become the Walter o'Dim of many manifestations.

Derry, ME

Derry's a runner-up to Castle Rock as the Number One Town.

The Running Man: With Amelia Williams as a willing hostage, Ben Richards negotiated for an airplane at Voigt Airfield near Derry.

"The Body": The Great Southern & Western Maine railroad ran up to Derry.

Pet Sematary: 1) Back in the day, loggers sent their product down the river to Derry. 2) Huey Garber's train dropped off a coffin in Derry before delivering Timmy Baterman's to Orrington.

"Mrs. Todd's Shortcut": Derry, specifically, isn't mentioned, but the Old Derry Road and Derry Hospital are given.

"Uncle Otto's Truck": Uncle Otto's father prospered in the Derry lumber industry.

IT: IT has terrorized Derry's children for a very long time.

The Tommyknockers: 1) Vera Anderson (no known relation to Bobbi) lived in Derry. When she visited a friend in Haven, her metal leg braces helped her resist the effects of becoming a Tommyknocker. 2) Patricia McArdle and Jim Gardener butted heads. Patricia was from Derry. 3) Ruth and Ralph McCausland lived in Derry before moving to Haven. 4) Hester Brookline and Tommy Jacklin went to Derry for batteries. 5) Troopers Bent and Rhodes, from the Derry barracks, disappeared.

The Dark Half: Liz Beaumont mentioned the Derry Animal Shelter.

"Secret Window, Secret Garden": The Mortons lived at 92 Kansas Street in Derry.

Needful Things: Sonny Jackett was the best mechanic outside Derry.

Gerald's Game: Law enforcement from several jurisdictions, including Derry, investigated cemetery desecration in western Maine. They called the perp "Rudolph."

Dolores Claiborne: In Little Tall's *The Weekly Tide*, Nosy Nettie wrote about Philo Caron coming from Derry to help his brother, John, caulk the *Deepstar*.

Insomnia: Ralph Roberts saved Patrick Danville in Derry.

Bag of Bones: The Noonans lived in Derry.

Hearts in Atlantis: Five carloads of University of Maine students protested the Vietnam War in front of the Federal Building in

Derry. Carol Gerber could be seen in the background in a Derry *News* photo.

Dreamcatcher: Beaver, Henry Devlin, Duddits, Jonesy, and Pete Moore grew up in Derry.

"Autopsy Room Four": Howard Cottrell escaped his autopsy in Derry.

"The Road Virus Heads North": Successful horror novelist Richard Kinnell lived (and died?) in Derry.

Lisey's Story: To keep Canty and Darla out of harm's way, Amanda Debusher fibbed that she was getting tests at Acadia Mental Health in Derry.

"Mute": Monette picked up a hitchhiker 160 miles from Derry.

Under the Dome: 1) Officer Henry Morrison and Sada Wheeler, short-order cook Anson's wife, had family in Derry. 2) Hannah Compton led the Lady Wildcats to a championship victory over the Castle Rock Rockets at the Derry Civic Center.

"Fair Extension": George Elvid gave Dave Streeter a fair extension in Derry.

11/22/63: The Dunnings lived in Derry.

Gwendy's Magic Feather: a nearby town to Castle Rock

"On Slide Inn Road": On their way to Derry to see Nan, the Brown family ran into trouble on Slide Inn Road.

"Rat": The day after Autumn Storm Pierre stopped and Drew Larson had helped clear the road from his cabin, Drew drove home. Instead of stopping for the night in Derry, he pushed on.

Gwendy's Final Task: 1) The Bradley Gang was massacred in the 1930s. 2) Ryan Brown was killed in a hit-and-run in 2019.

Flint City, OK

The Outsider: Terry Maitland was attending a teacher's conference in Cap City at the same time he was brutalizing a boy in Flint City.

"If It Bleeds": Ralph Anderson and family of Flint City vacationed in the Bahamas.

French Landing, WI

Black House: The Fisherman killed French Landing children.

The Dark Tower: Walter wore a hoodie he picked up in an abandoned house in French Landing.

Gates Center, ME

Sword in the Darkness: Twin sisters from Gates Center went to school in Gates Falls.

"It Grows on You": On Thursday afternoons, Cora Newell shopped at the Kitty Korner Store in Gates Center.

Gates Falls, ME

While Castle Rock is Stephen King's Number One Town, Gates Falls is his Number One Sidekick Town. Other than a couple of short stories, it isn't the primary scene of action, but it shows up as a nearby town over and over again.

Sword in the Darkness: Miss Edie Rowsmith's teaching career started in Gates Falls. Her relationship with Don Knowles ended in tragedy.

'Salem's Lot: While most of the action takes place in Jerusalem's Lot, nearby Gates Falls gets some love: 1) Gates Bank and Trust experienced a run in 1930. 2) The body of a hit-and-run victim was found off Route 116. 3) George Boyer, Harriet and Lester Durham, David Evans, Grover Merrill, and Mickey Sylvester worked at Gates Mill and Weaving.

Rage: John Dano, one of the kids held in the classroom, lived in Gates Falls.

"Graveyard Shift": A crew found rats while cleaning the basement and sub-cellar of a textile mill in Gates Falls.

The Dead Zone: Tom Harrison became chief of the Gates Falls police after taking a Rural Law Enforcement course with Frank Dodd at the University of Colorado.

"Stud City": Johnny May's Dodge would run fast on the road from Gates Falls to Castle Rock.

"Mrs. Todd's Shortcut": The auctioneer in Gates Falls talked fast.

"Gramma": Uncle George's wife and three daughters Christmas-shopped in Gates Falls.

The Dark Half: You can get to Castle Rock by getting off the turnpike at Gates Falls.

Needful Things: Principal Frank Jewett picked up his adult magazines from the post office in Gates Falls.

"It Grows on You": Cora and Joe Newall lived in Gates Falls, where Joe made his fortune, before moving to Castle Rock.

Bag of Bones: Sara and the Red-Top Boys had performed in Gates Falls and other western Maine towns.

Hearts in Atlantis: Hearts addict Pete Riley hailed from Gates Falls.

The Plant: Zenith House editor Bill Gelb grew up in Gates Falls.

"Riding the Bullet": An old man gave the hitchhiking Alan Parker a ride as far as Gates Falls.

Revival: Patsy and Morrie Jacobs were heading to the Red & White Market in Gates Falls when they were killed on Sirois Hill.

Gwendy's Button Box: Gwendy Peterson and Harry Streeter's first date was at the Gates Falls Roller Rink.

"Mr. Harrigan's Phone": Middle school and high school kids from neighboring tuition towns went to school in Gates Falls.

"Rat": Bran Larson choked on a cherry tomato at Country Kitchen. Drew Larson's quickness with the Heimlich Maneuver saved him.

Gatlin, NE

"Children of the Corn": The kids of Gatlin worshipped He Who Walks Behind the Rows.

IT: Ben Hanscom lived on a farm in Junkins, NE, outside Hemingford Home and near Gatlin.

Gretna, ME

"The Revenge of Lard Ass Hogan": Gretna, ME, residents had annual pie-eating contests.

"Nona": People from Castle Rock, Gretna, and Harlow enjoyed the Oxford Plains stock-car races. Every night resulted in a parking-lot fight.

Harding

Sword in the Darkness: Webs McCullough and his gang started a race riot to deflect from their robbing illicit drug and loan-shark operations.

The Running Man: Ben Richards hailed from Harding's Co-Op City.

Harlow, South Harlow, and West Harlow, ME

Derry's a runner-up to Gates Falls as the Number One Sidekick Town.

'Salem's Lot: In a deleted scene, Parker Crockett [renamed Larry Crockett] hired two haulers from Harlow.

Rage: The Deckers lived between Windsor and Harlow.

"The Body": A GS&WM train hit and killed Ray Brower near Back Harlow Road in South Harlow.

"Nona": The Hollises lived in Harlow, across the river from Castle Rock.

"Uncle Otto's Truck": Uncle Otto and George McCutcheon bought 4,000 acres of New England Paper land cheap. The parcel was mostly in Castle Rock, but stretched into Harlow and Waterford.

The Dark Half: One of Castle Rock's Little League fields was near Harlow.

Gerald's Game: Charles Sutlin bought Prince for his daughter, Cathy, at a roadside stand in Harlow. Then, to avoid a $70 dog tax if he brought him home, he dumped the dog in the woods.

Bag of Bones: Jo Noonan talked with folks in Harlow and Motton about Dark Score Lake's dark past.

"Riding the Bullet": Alan Parker and his mother lived in Harlow.

Lisey's Story: The Deep Cut Road went to Harlow.

Blaze: Blaze and other Hetton House boys raked blueberries for Harry Bluenote in West Harlow.

"N.": Dr. Johnny Bonsaint and his sister, Sheila, went to the Ackerman School in Harlow.

Under the Dome: Harlow bordered Chester's Mill to the east and northeast.

Revival: Jamie Morton grew up in and met Charlie Jacobs in Harlow.

"Drunken Fireworks": Alden McCausland's father, a skilled carpenter, died of a heart attack at a job-site in Harlow.

"Mr. Harrigan's Phone": Craig called Mr. Harrigan's iPhone in Harlow.

Harrison State Park in Maine

Rage: Charlie Decker and Joe McKennedy took Annmarie and Rosalynn to a Harrison State Park picnic. Charlie vomited in Joe's car.

"Night Surf": Bernie's mother took him and his friends to the park.

"The Body": Gordie and Denny Lachance body-surfed at Harrison.

"N.": Amateur photographer N. snapped pictures at Harrison State Park.

Harwich, CT

Hearts in Atlantis: Carol Gerber, Bobby Garfield, Willie Shearman, and Sully-John grew up in Harwich. Breaker Ted Brautigan stayed a bit with the Garfields.

The Dark Tower: On their way to New York City, Roland and Mrs. Tassenbaum spent the night in a Motel 6.

Haven, ME

Haven naming history: In 1813, Hugh Crane bought a tract of land from the Commonwealth of Massachusetts. Three years later, it earned municipal status and became known as Montville Plantation. In 1831, Montville Plantation became Coodersville, due, perhaps, to businessmen George and Hiram Cooder. During the Civil War, Ellis Montgomery died fighting with the 20th Maine at Gettysburg. On 4 July 1864, they renamed Coodersville to Montgomery. In 1878, the townspeople changed the name to Ilium to fit in with other classically named towns. Later, Ilium became Haven.

Pet Sematary: Tremont Withers was from Haven.

"Mrs. Todd's Shortcut": A Castle Rock-to-Bangor shortcut passed through Haven.

IT: 1) Eddie Kaspbrak had an aunt in Haven. 2) There was a Derry-Newport-Haven interurban bus. 3) Claude Heroux set fire to Haven's Big Injun Woods. 4) Rebecca Paulson lived in Haven Village.

The Tommyknockers: Bobbi Anderson found something big buried on her Haven property.

The Stand: A Haven woman wrote *Rimfire Christmas*, a Western.

Insomnia: 1) Ed Deepneau flew over South Haven on his way to disrupt the Susan Day rally in Derry. 2) In his state of hyper-reality, Ralph Roberts *saw* telephone conversations, including one about a Haven farmer.

11/22/63: Harry Dunning lived with his aunt and uncle in Haven after his father killed the rest of his family.

Hemingford Home, NE

The Stand: Mother Abagail lived most of her one hundred eight years in Hemingford Home, Polk County, NE.

"The Last Rung on the Ladder": Katrina and Larry grew up on a three-hundred-acre corn-and-cattle farm in Hemingford Home.

IT: Ben Hanscom lived on a farm in Junkins, NE, outside Hemingford Home and near Gatlin.

"1922": The James family—Arlette, Wilfred, and Henry—lived on a Hemingford Home farm.

"Afterlife": Bill Andrews was born in Hemingford County Hospital.

"Mister Yummy": Hemingford Home is in Hemingford County.

Billy Summers: Billy and Alice Maxwell talked on a dirt road in Hemingford Home.

Jerusalem's Lot, ME

'Salem's Lot: We learn the most about Jerusalem's Lot in this novel.

"Jerusalem's Lot": This short story shows us the Lot's attraction to evil long before Hubie Marsten and Kurt Barlow.

"One for the Road": The town's vampire problem isn't over.

The Dead Zone: After her stroke, Vera Smith was sent to Cumberland General near Jerusalem's Lot.

"The Body": When discussing the stupid sounding name Gordie Lachance chose for the name of the town in his "The Revenge of Lard Ass Hogan"—Gretna—Chris Chambers remarked that real Maine towns, such as Jerusalem's Lot and Castle Rock, sounded just as stupid.

Pet Sematary: Heading north on the Maine Turnpike, Exit 12 led to Falmouth, Cumberland, and Jerusalem's Lot.

Dolores Claiborne: The village being so empty for the eclipse reminded Dolores of that town "where they say no one lives."

"The Night Flier": Maine's Cumberland County Airport sat between Falmouth and the mostly deserted town of Jerusalem's Lot. [Note: The Jerusalem's Lot reference was edited out of the version in *Nightmares & Dreamscapes*.]

Dreamcatcher: Exit 9 of the southbound side of the turnpike led to Falmouth, Cumberland, and Jerusalem's Lot.

The Dark Tower: 1) Pere Callahan had fled Jerusalem's Lot in a world other than that of Calla Bryn Sturgis. 2) The Keystone World had no such town as it was a fictional creation.

Doctor Sleep: Jerusalem's Lot was one of several safe havens for the True Knot.

Revival: Looking east from Skytop, one could see Brunswick, Freeport, and Jerusalem's Lot.

The Institute: Forty or so years ago, the people of Jerusalem's Lot disappeared.

Junction City, IA

"The Library Policeman": Sam Peebles dealt with Ardelia Lortz in Junction City.

Needful Things: After Castle Rock, Leland Gaunt opened a shop in Junction City.

Kashwakamak Township (Kashwak), ME

Bag of Bones: Along with Harlow, Motton, and TR-90, Kashwakamak was in southern Castle County.

"The Man in the Black Suit": Castle Stream forked in Motton. One branch flowed to Castle Rock, the other to Kashwakamak Township.

Cell: The phone-crazies sent the normies to the Northern Counties Expo fairgrounds in Kashwakamak.

Kashwakamak Lake in Maine

Gerald's Game: Kashwakamak Lake is near Tashmore Glen.

Cell: The Lake is also near Kashwakamak.

Keywadin Pond in Maine

Bag of Bones: Dave Stanchfield died when he accidentally drove his pulp-truck into Keywadin Pond in Lovell.

The Dark Tower: Keywadin Pond bordered East Stoneham, ME.

Note: Lovell and Stoneham are about six miles apart.

La Plata, TX

While Texas has a La Plata, it's a ghost town. King's La Plata is a fully populated fictional town.

IT: *IT* doesn't mention the town by name, but calls out a Texas city with a disproportionately low rate of violent crime because of something in the water.

"The End of the Whole Mess": Richard Fornoy discovered that a protein in the water of La Plata had a calming effect on people. His grand plan to calm the world backfired.

the Plains of Leng

The Eyes of the Dragon: Flagg had a book of spells Alhazred had written on the Plains of Leng.

Needful Things: Leland Gaunt gave Ace Merrill a cocaine hybrid from the Plains of Leng.

Little Tall Island, ME

Dolores Claiborne: Dolores lived and worked on Little Tall.

"Home Delivery": Little Tall Island had two cemeteries, while Jenny Island had one.

Storm of the Century: Andre Linoge came to Little Tall and promised to go away if they gave him what he wanted.

Los Zapatos, Mexico

'Salem's Lot: Ben Mears and Mark Petrie lived in Los Zapatos for several months before returning to Jerusalem's Lot.

The Dark Tower: Black Thirteen sent Donald Callahan todash to Los Zapatos for Ben Mears's funeral.

the City of Lud

The Dark Tower: Roland's ka-tet traveled through Lud.

Rose Madder: Dorcas had been to the City of Lud.

Ludlow, ME

Pet Sematary: The kids of Ludlow buried lost animals in the Pet Sematary. Beyond the Sematary, was another cemetery of sorts, in land the Micmac Indians felt had soured.

The Tommyknockers: Micmac Chief Wahwayvokah declared the Great Woods, aka Big Injun Woods, which stretched from Ludlow, cursed.

The Dark Half: The Beaumonts lived in Ludlow.

Insomnia: Lois Chasse played nickel-dime poker with the girls in Ludlow.

Mile 81 Rest Area on the Maine Turnpike (I-95)

Dreamcatcher: Mr. Gray stopped at the Mile 81 rest area.

"Mile 81": A car parked on the entrance ramp, attracted Good Samaritans, and ate them.

Motton, ME

Motton is another sidekick town.

Carrie: 1) Margaret Brigham, Carrie's mother, was raised in Motton. Margaret's father, John Brigham, was shot and killed in his bar, The Jolly Roadhouse, outside Motton. 2) The Whites' next-door neighbor, Stella Horan, took courses at Lewin Business College in Motton. 3) Fire departments from Motton and other nearby towns assisted Chamberlain on Prom Night. Injured were taken to Motton Receiving Hospital. 4) As Ewen Consolidated High School's gymnasium was destroyed on Prom Night, surviving seniors held graduation ceremonies at Motton Academy.

"The Body": Ray Brower was from Chamberlain, near Motton.

Gerald's Game: 1) A path around Kashwakamak Lake headed toward Motton. 2) Raymond Andrew Joubert had lived with his stepmother and her common-law husband in Motton. They abused him, so he killed them and ate much of the husband.

"It Grows on You": Joe Newall hired a guy from Motton to run his small dairy business after buying sixteen cows and a milking machine.

Bag of Bones: Jo Noonan talked with folks in Harlow and Motton about Dark Score Lake's dark past.

The Girl Who Loved Tom Gordon: Search teams looked for Trish McFarland in the woods around Motton and TR-90. She had crossed into New Hampshire.

"The Man in the Black Suit": Gary encountered the Devil on the bank of Castle Stream in Motton.

Lisey's Story: Smiley Flanders, the Landons' plumber, lived in Motton.

"N.": Ackerman's Field, N.'s obsession, was in Motton.

Under the Dome: Motton bordered Chester's Mill to the south and southeast.

Revival: Norm Irving's father lived in a Motton trailer park. Norm was the leader of Chrome Roses, the band in which Jamie Morton played rhythm guitar.

"Mr. Harrigan's Phone": In 2008, Motton had Harlow's closest cell phone tower.

Oatley, NY

The Talisman: Jack Sawyer had no trouble getting into Oakley, but struggled getting out.

"The Sun Dog": Kevin Delevan dreamed of walking into Oatley. A bum called him a fushing feef. The circumstances of the dream mirrored Jack Sawyer's entry into Oatley.

Black House: Memories of Oatley returned to a grown-up Jack Sawyer.

Paradise Falls, OH

Christine: George LeBay, Roland's brother, was from Paradise Falls.

The Talisman: Jack Sawyer escaped paid sex with Emory W. Light, who lived in Paradise Falls and was the First Mercantile Bank of Paradise Falls President.

Rocksburg, PA

Christine: Regina Cunningham grew up in Rocksburg.

From a Buick 8: Rocksburg neighbored Statler Township. Ned Wilcox hit two home runs against the Rocksburg Railroad, a Legion baseball team.

Note: Rocksburg, PA, is also the fictional town in a series of K. C. Constantine mysteries featuring Mario Balzik.

Shiloh, ME

"The Body": For a good time, Ace Merrill and friends would steal a car and take their girlfriends drinking and parking in Castle View, Harlow, or Shiloh.

"Mr. Harrigan's Phone": Shiloh Church was one of several tuition towns from which kids went to Gates Falls Middle.

Shooter's Knob, TN

"Secret Window, Secret Garden": Ted Milner, Amy Rainey's new love interest, was from Shooter's Knob.

Lisey's Story: John Doolin, alias Jim Dooley, was born here.

Sidewinder, CO

The Shining: The Overlook Hotel was forty miles west of Sidewinder, the nearest town.

The Talisman: The Pit in the Territories reminded Jack Sawyer of an open-pit molybdenum mine outside Sidewinder.

Misery: Annie Wilkes picked up the hitchhiking Andrew Pomeroy on his way to Sidewinder to sketch the ruins of the Overlook Hotel. When she found he was no artist, she killed him with an ax.

American Vampire: Fortune-hunting divers inadvertently freed the undead Skinner Sweet from the flooded Sidewinder.

Doctor Sleep: Sidewinder was one of several safe havens for the True Knot.

Billy Summers: Billy and Alice Maxwell visited Bucky Hanson, hiding out in Sidewinder.

Stovington, VT

The Shining: The Torrances lived in Stovington, and Jack taught English at Stovington Preparatory Academy.

The Stand: Stu Redman escaped from the Stovington Plague Center.

The Dead Zone: Chuck Chatsworth spent a year at Stovington Prep in Vermont. Note: the town of Stovington is not mentioned.

"Everything's Eventual": Billy Unger, one of Dinky Earnshaw's targets, lived in Stovington.

Tarker's Mills, ME

Cycle of the Werewolf: Uncle Al helped Marty Coslaw stop the Beast, a werewolf, from terrorizing Tarker's Mills.

Under the Dome: Chester's Mill and Tarker's Mills together were called the Twin Mills.

Tashmore Glen (Tashmore) and Tashmore Pond, ME

"Secret Window, Secret Garden": The Raineys had a summer home on Tashmore Lake in Tashmore Glen.

Gerald's Game: The Burlingames had a summer home on Kashwakamak Lake near Tashmore Glen.

The Colorado Kid: Six of eight people died from drinking poisoned iced coffee at a Methodist Church picnic at Tashmore Lake. This remains one of the region's popular unsolved mysteries.

Cell: High school kids around Kashwakamak were bused to Tashmore.

Lisey's Story: A winter storm took out the power in several Castle County towns, including Tashmore Pond.

TR-90, ME

Bag of Bones: The Noonans had a summer home on TR-90's Dark Score Lake. There was a big to-do about Sara Tidwell almost a hundred years after her murder.

The Girl Who Loved Tom Gordon: Search teams looked for Trish McFarland in the woods around Motton and TR-90. She had crossed into New Hampshire.

Cell: Kashwakamak was in this unincorporated area.

Under the Dome: The TR-90 Unincorporated Township bordered Chester's Mill to the north. Oldtimers called it Canton.

"Drunken Fireworks": For the last Fourth of July Arms race, cars lined roads toward TR–90 and Chester's Mill.

"Rat": Drew Larson went to his father's cabin in TR–90 to write a novel. After three failed attempts, he hoped the fourth time would be a charm.

TR-100, ME

Bag of Bones: Max Devore owned land in TR-100 and TR-110, across Dark Score Lake from TR-90.

The Girl Who Loved Tom Gordon: one of three incorporated townships near New Hampshire

TR-110, ME

Bag of Bones: Max Devore owned land in TR-100 and TR-110, across Dark Score Lake from TR-90.

The Girl Who Loved Tom Gordon: one of three incorporated townships near New Hampshire

The Institute: The Institute's American compound was in TR-110, in the boondocks of Maine.

Wentworth, OH

Desperation: Some of Tak's unfortunate victims were travelers from Wentworth.

The Regulators: Tak used Seth Garin to terrorize Wentworth.

Organization Connections

249B East Thirty-Fifth Street

"The Breathing Method", "The Man Who Would Not Shake Hands": This was a gentlemen's club of sorts. Part of another world, it had many entrances and exits. The upstairs contained so many rooms and corridors that a person could get lost. Shelves held books found nowhere else in our world. Unknown companies manufactured various furnishings. Thursdays were story nights, with the Thursday before Christmas saved for special uncanny tales. "IT IS THE TALE, NOT HE WHO TELLS IT"

longtime host: Stevens

members: David Adley, Peter Andrews, George Gregson, Johanssen, Emlyn McCarron

Acadia Mental Health Hospital

Insomnia: Derry's Charlie Pickering was in this and other hospitals for mental issues.

Lisey's Story: Acadia Mental Health is in Derry, ME.

"Fair Extension": Another Acadia Mental Health was in Bangor, ME.

Arrowhead

"The Mist": The Arrowhead Project may have caused the mist with deadly out-of-this-world creatures.

The Tommyknockers: The Arrowhead installation in Maine, with its nuclear reactor, caused a few protests.

Blue Ribbon Laundry

Carrie: Margaret White worked at the Blue Ribbon Laundry in Chamberlain Center.

"The Mangler": The Blue Ribbon Laundry's 30' x 6' Hadley-Watson Model-6 Speed Ironer and Folder killed two people and injured three others after a demon possessed it.

Roadwork: Barton Dawes worked for the Blue Ribbon Laundry on Fir Street in Western. The steam ironer and folder was called the mangler.

[Easter Egg] "Rita Hayworth and Shawshank Redemption": Although not a Blue Ribbon, Shawshank State Prison's laundry had a steam ironer and folder called the mangler.

the Bridgton Pharmacy

"The King Family and the Wicked Witch": Witch Hazel bought Daddy's books at the pharmacy.

Cujo: Vic Trenton bought toy trucks at the pharmacy for Tad Trenton's collection.

"The Mist": David Drayton and others had a harrowing experience at the pharmacy. The pharmacy shared a shopping center with a Federal Foods Supermarket and the Norge Washateria (a coin-op laundry).

Dreamcatcher: Trish bought aspirin for a headache before giving a presentation at work.

[Easter Egg] A Bridgton shopping center in *The Dark Tower* had a supermarket, a laundry, and a drugstore.

Cheery Petroleum Company

The Stand: The Trashcan Man set fire to Cheery Petroleum Company's #1 storage tank.

The Outsider: Peter Maitland worked for Cheery Petroleum Company.

Daughters and Sisters (D&S)

Rose Madder: A group of women who helped battered women.

Desperation: Cynthia Smith had become a counselor at D&S.

the Chester's Mill *Democrat*

"N.": Julia Shumway wrote an article for the *Democrat*.

Under the Dome: Julia Shumway ran the *Democrat*, as did her father, grandfather, and great-grandfather before her.

Federal Foods, Inc.

"The Mist": Federal Foods, Inc., was the parent company of the Federal Foods Supermarket.

Blaze: Harry Bluenote sold blueberries to Federal Foods, Inc., and other food companies.

Finders Keepers

Finders Keepers: Bill Hodges and Holly Gibney ran Finders Keepers, an unofficial Private Investigation firm.

End of Watch: Bill Hodges left Finders Keepers to Holly Gibney in his will.

The Outsider: Alec Pelley called Finders Keepers and retained Holly Gibney for an investigation.

Four Fathers

"The Ballad of the Flexible Bullet": Henry Wilson blacked out after drinking at Four Fathers.

The Plant: John Kenton and Roger Wade had a drink at Four Fathers, owned by *mafioso* Ginelli.

The Dark Tower: Balazar associate Ginelli ran Four Fathers.

the Great Southern and Western Maine (GS&WM) Railroad

"The Body": The boys followed the GS&WM tracks to find the body.

"Nona": The narrator saw a GS&WM trestle upstream from where he dumped Norman Blanchette's body.

Cycle of the Werewolf: The Beast killed Arnie Westrum, a GS&WM flagman.

IT: The GS&WM ran through Derry.

Insomnia: The GS&WM ran past Derry County Airport.

Joyland: The last freight train ran past South Berwick, ME, around 1963.

Horlicks University

"The Crate": Much of "The Crate" took place at Horlicks University, a school founded over a hundred forty years before. The creature in the crate disposed of janitor Mike Latimer.

"The Raft": The kids on the raft on Cascade Lake—Deke, Laverne, Rachel, and Randy—went to Horlicks University.

Christine: 1) Regina Cunningham was an English professor, and Michael Cunningham a history professor. 2) Uncle Fred was a janitor and mentioned another janitor had disappeared. 3) Dennis's mother took a writing course.

From a Buick 8: To support his examination and dissection of the bat-thing, Curt Wilcox borrowed equipment from the Biology Department at Horlicks University.

Inside View

The supermarket tabloid published in New York had a weekly circulation of three million.

> reporter: Rick Dees
>
> psychics under contract: Tim Clark, Kathy Nolan, Frank Ross, and others

The Dead Zone: This book introduces us to *Inside View.*

Needful Things: Nettie Cobb read *Inside View*.

"The Night Flier": Rick Dees followed a Cessna-flying vampire for *Inside View*.

"Popsy": a cheap weekly tabloid

"Home Delivery": *Inside View* was the first to cover zombies in America, specifically, Thumper, FL.

Insomnia: *Inside View* ads sold wacky insomnia remedies.

Desperation: Johnny Marinville's beating up his wife made *Inside View*'s center-spread.

Bag of Bones: 1) Mike Noonan thought Devore family drama would be perfect material for *Inside View.* 2) Mike worked on a novel so intensely that *Inside View* could write about Jo Noonan's affair with Tom Selleck and he wouldn't notice.

From a Buick 8: Pump-jockey Bradley Roach was reading *Inside View* when a man abandoned the Buick at the Jenny station in Statler Township, PA.

The Dark Tower: Mrs. Greta Shaw read *Inside View*. Eddie Dean didn't believe their stories.

"Big Driver": *Inside View* would report the more sordid details of Tessa Jean's sexual assault if they got wind of it.

Joyland: The tabloid ran a special edition after Annie Ross shot Lane Hardy.

Doctor Sleep: The Stones didn't want Abra to be an *Inside View* cover story.

End of Watch: Holly Gibney sneaked Janice Ellerton's Zappit from the crime scene in an issue of *Inside View.*

Elevation: Scott Carey didn't want to be an *Inside View* star attraction.

"If It Bleeds": Holly Gibney thought *Inside View* would love her information on the many incarnations of Chet Ondowsky.

Billy Summers: Billy projected the image of a man who read *Inside View*, other tabloids, and comic books.

Joyland

Joyland: Dev Jones got a summer job at this amusement park on the ocean in Heaven's Bay, NC.

Revival: Charlie Jacobs performed as Mr. Electrico at this seaside amusement park in North Carolina.

Juniper Hill

IT: Henry Bowers transferred from Augusta State Mental Hospital to Juniper Hill, a mental hospital near Augusta for the criminally insane.

The Tommyknockers: an asylum in Juniper Hill

The Dark Half: The mental asylum wasn't all that far from Castle Rock.

"The Sun Dog": Kevin Delevan thought he'd be a good candidate for Juniper Hill if he talked about the Sun dog.

Needful Things: 1) Nettie Cobb spent five years in this mental institution near Augusta, ME, after killing her abusive husband. 2) Buster Keeton's uncle was in around the same time as Nettie. 3) Reverend Tom Killingsworth held services twice a week.

Gerald's Game: Raymond Andrew Joubert was sent here after his unspeakable acts on a six-year-old boy.

"Suffer the Little Children": They sent Miss Sidley to this Augusta institution after she killed twelve of her students she was sure were monsters masquerading as children.

Insomnia: Charlie Pickering had been in several mental health institutions, including this one.

Bag of Bones: If the supernatural stuff Mike Noonan got involved in wasn't real, he thought he'd be ready for Juniper Hill.

Cell: a madhouse in Augusta, ME

Gwendy's Final Task: A man was sent here after a clown made him kill his family.

Motokops 2200

Desperation: Kirsten Carver wore a *MotoKops 2200* shirt. Cassie Styles and Colonel Henry were her favorite cartoon characters.

The Regulators: *MotoKops 2200* was an NBC Saturday-morning cartoon epic featuring a team of MotoKops and their arch-enemies, all who drove futuristic Power Wagons. The show inspired action figures and other merchandise, such as clothing, bed sheets, and lunch boxes.

Nite Owl convenience store

"Gray Matter": Henry Parmalee ran a Nite Owl in Clifton, ME.

Thinner: A townsman started a fight with a Gypsy outside a Nite Owl in Attleboro, MA.

IT: A maple smashed the Nite Owl at the corner of Cape Avenue and Merit Street in the big storm.

Lisey's Story: Prior to a reading in Bowling Green, KY, Scott Landon sent a grad student to the Nite Owl for a bottle of Nyquil.

"Willa": David Sanderson asked whether Phil Palmer wanted him to get a pack of cigarettes from a Nite Owl or 7-Eleven in Crowheart Springs, WY.

the Organization

"Before the Play": Vito Gienelli was high in the Organization.

"Battleground": They contracted John Renshaw to kill Hans Morris.

"The Ledge": Cressner was an organized-crime leader with the Organization.

The Stand: Dewey the Deck dealt marijuana and cocaine. He avoided heroin to not cross the Organization.

Firestarter: The Shop sold them heroin.

Roadwork: Barton Dawes thought Sal Magliore might have been a member.

Orinco

Pet Sematary: An Orinco truck is the source of tragedy.

IT: An Orinco chemical-fertilizer truck passed Richie Tozier on his way back to Derry.

The Dark Half: An Orinco truck blew past the Beaumont's Ludlow home on Route 15.

the Overlook Hotel

The Shining: The Overlook Hotel is the villain in *The Shining*.

Misery: Annie Wilkes picked up the hitchhiking Andrew Pomeroy on his way to Sidewinder to sketch the ruins of the Overlook Hotel.

Doctor Sleep: The True Knot owned the Bluebell Campground on the site of the former Overlook Hotel.

Billy Summers: A mile-long path in the woods behind Bucky Hanson's log house led to a gorge, across which one could see a clearing where the Overlook Hotel once stood.

Portland General Hospital

Cycle of the Werewolf: Donna Lee Sturmfeller was treated after "falling down the stairs" after her husband, Milt, hit her.

Blaze: Blaze was in a coma for three weeks after his father threw him down the apartment stairs three times.

Quik-Flash convenience store

11/22/63: After George Amberson gummed up the works, an abandoned Quik-Flash stood in place of Al's Diner.

"Herman Wouk Is Still Alive": The Quik-Flash chain went out of business.

Quik-Pik convenience store

The Dead Zone: There was a Quik-Pik in Durham, NH.

Blaze: Tim and Janet Quarles ran a Quik-Pik in Maine. Blaze robbed it twice.

Billy Summers: Alice Maxwell and Billy stopped at a Quik-Pik in Nevada.

Serenity Hill

"N.": Dr. Bonsaint's psychiatrist-mentor was Chief of Staff in Augusta.

"Mute": Hitchhiker Stanley Doucette had been in and out of this mental institution near Augusta, ME.

Shawshank State Prison, aka The Shank

"Rita Hayworth and Shawshank Redemption": After twenty-seven years, Andy Dufresne escaped from Shawshank State Prison.

"The Body": Chris Chambers tried to break up a fight at the Chicken Delight in Portland. One guy, who had been in Shawshank State Prison just a week before, stabbed and killed him.

IT: 1) Two avoid two years in the Shank, Butch Bowers paid Will Hanlon $200 for poisoning Will's chickens. 2) Steven Dubay got fifteen years at Shawshank State Prison for his involvement in the death of Adrian Mellon. 3) One of Cheryl Lamonica's boyfriends was an armed-robbery convict in Shawshank. 4) Richard P. Macklin got a two-to-ten-year sentence for the murder of Dorsey Corcoran, his stepson. 5) Father Ashley O'Brian was a Shawshank priest.

"The Fifth Quarter": Barney and the fifth quarter met in the Shank.

"The Sun Dog": Ace Merrill spent four years here.

Needful Things: Ace Merrill got four years at the Shawshank Prison.

Bag of Bones: Jared Devore persuaded Ben Merrill to kill Kito Tidwell so they wouldn't spend forty years in Shawshank for what they did to Sara Tidwell.

Dreamcatcher: While the abandoned Tracker Brothers office in Jonesy's mind was cramped, it was bigger than a Shawshank cell.

Blaze: 1) If Blaze were caught robbing Tim & Janet's Quik-Pik, he'd go to Shawshank. 2) If Blaze kept doing small-time stuff, he'd wind up in the Shank. 3) Anne Bradstay's boyfriend got six years in Shawshank State Prison for French-fryin'—burning warehouses.

Under the Dome: 1) To keep out of Shawshank State Prison after severely beating Angie McCain, Junior Rennie killed her. 2) Confessing his sin of producing crystal meth would lead Big Jim to Shawshank. 3) Aidan Appleton wore a "PROPERTY OF SHAWSHANK STATE PRISON" T-shirt.

"A Good Marriage": When Darcy discovered his secret, Bob Anderson thought he could end up in Shawshank.

11/22/63: Frank Dunning died in the prison after killing most of his family.

Gwendy's Magic Feather: Castle Rock farmer Henderson may have served time.

"Mr. Harrigan's Phone": Mr. Harrigan's Harlow mansion was known as the Big House, as was Shawshank Prison.

"On Slide Inn Road": Two men had killed a woman and would surely go to the Shank if caught.

the Shop

Firestarter: The Shop sponsored Dr. Wanless's Lot Six experiments then monitored and eliminated all those who showed paranormal skills.

The Stand: The Shop handled the Project Blue cover-up and containment after Captain Trips got out.

The Tommyknockers: The Shop covered up Haven's Tommyknocker problem.

"The Langoliers": a shadowy government organization

Shopwell supermarket

The Long Walk: The Walkers passed a Shopwell in Maine on their first night.

Bag of Bones: The Derry strip mall where Jo Noonan suffered a brain aneurysm contained a Shopwell.

Sleeping Beauties: Part-time dealer of medicinal drugs Norma Bradshaw worked in the produce department of the Shopwell in Dooling.

The Outsider: Howie Gold lightheartedly suggested garlic from Shopwell to repel the outsider.

the Sombra Corporation

The Dark Tower: A corporate entity that supported the Crimson King, they opposed Roland Deschain's efforts to save the Tower.

Gwendy's Final Task: The Sombra Corporation enlisted Gareth Winston to steal Gwendy's button box.

Stovington Preparatory Academy

The Shining: Jack Torrance taught English until he was fired for beating up George Hatfield for letting the air out of his tires.

The Dead Zone: Tutor Johnny Smith recommended Chuck Chatsworth spend a year at Stovington Prep between high school and college.

Doctor Sleep: Jack Torrance had an affair with a student.

the Tet Corporation

The Dark Tower: The Tet Corporation became a bigger deal than North Central Positronics.

Gwendy's Final Task: TetCorp ran a rocket launch facility in Playalinda, FL.

Zoney's GoMart/Go-Mart

A Zoney's GoMart convenience store featured prominently in Kelly Braffert's *Save Yourself*. Paying homage, Uncle Stevie turned it into a chain. Ms. Braffert is Owen King's wife.

Mr. Mercedes: Barbara Robinson and friends hung out.

Finders Keepers: Zoney's sponsored the Zebras, a Little League team.

Sleeping Beauties: The Zoney's in Dooling, WV, sold gasoline.

The Outsider: A Zoney's Go-Mart was across the street from the police station.

Elevation: A Zoney's Go-Mart was on the Turkey Trot 12K route.

The Institute: Zoney's Go-Mart was the only 24-hour store in DuPray, SC.

"Mr. Harrigan's Phone": Drunk driver Dean Whitmore lost his license after ramming into the side of the Zoney's in Hingham, MA.

"The Life of Chuck": When Chuck Krantz lived with his grandparents, there was a Zoney's down the street.

Billy Summers: Billy walked past two guys who then robbed a Zoney's in Red Bluff.

Character Connections

Mother Abagail

The Stand: Mother Abagail lived in Hemingford Home, NE. People dreamed of her and travelled to see her.

The Dark Tower: People dreamed of Abagail, an old woman in Nebraska.

Abbalah

The Plant: Dark arts aficionado Carlos Detweiller worshipped Abbalah.

Black House: the Crimson King

Derek Anderson

The Outsider: Derek was away at a camp in Michigan while his father and others dealt with the outsider.

"If It Bleeds": During a teachers' strike, Derek and his family vacationed in the Bahamas.

Detective Ralph Anderson

The Outsider: The detective, Holly Gibney, and others tracked the outsider.

"If It Bleeds": Ralph and his family vacationed in the Bahamas.

Roberta Anderson

See the Famous Writer Connections chapter.

Mrs. Cora Babineau

End of Watch: Brady Hartsfield entered Dr. Babineau's mind, took control, and killed Mrs. Babineau.

The Outsider: The news reported that Dr. Babineau went off the deep end and murdered his wife.

Dr. Felix Babineau

Mr. Mercedes: Dr. Babineau treated Brady Hartsfield at the Lakes Region Traumatic Brain Injury Clinic of Kiner Memorial Hospital.

Finders Keepers: Dr. Babineau continued treating Brady Hartsfield.

End of Watch: Brady Hartsfield entered Dr. Babineau's mind and took complete control.

The Outsider: The news reported that Dr. Babineau went off the deep end, murdered his wife, and was killed in a shoot-out.

Sheriff George F. Bannerman

The Dead Zone: Johnny Smith led Sheriff Bannerman to the Castle Rock Strangler.

Cujo: The Sheriff died trying to save Donna Trenton and Tad Trenton from the rabid dog in Joe Camber's dooryard.

"The Body": Bannerman was the constable in 1960.

The Dark Half: George was sheriff during two national-newsworthy events in Castle Rock.

"The Sun Dog": The Author's Note revealed that George Bannerman had his first intimate encounter in his father's car.

Needful Things: A rabid dog had killed Joe Camber and Sheriff George Bannerman.

Gwendy's Button Box: The Sheriff investigated the collapse of the Suicide Stairs.

Elevation: Part of Route 119 was renamed Bannerman Road after Castle Rock's longest-serving sheriff.

Gwendy's Magic Feather: A rabid Saint Bernard killed the Sheriff and others.

Katrina Bannerman

The Dead Zone: Sheriff Bannerman's daughter might have been a Castle Rock Strangler victim had she crossed the Common alone, without classmate Sue Flaharty.

Cujo: Katrina narrowly escaped being Frank Dodd's victim.

Kurt Barlow

'Salem's Lot: Jerusalem's Lot suffered Kurt Barlow.

The Dark Tower: Barlow was a Type One vampire.

Elizabeth Stephens Beaumont

The Dark Half: Wife of the novelist Thaddeus Beaumont, she suggested he write under a pseudonym to overcome writer's block.

Needful Things: Thad's wife and twins left him after he became a drunk.

Thaddeus Beaumont

See the Famous Writer Connections chapter.

Wendy and William Beaumont

The Dark Half: Liz and Thad's twin children

Needful Things: Thad's wife and twins left him after he became a drunk.

Morris Randolph Bellamy

Finders Keepers: Morris was fascinated with John Rothstein's Jimmy Gold trilogy.

The Outsider: Morris Bellamy murdered his favorite author.

Blaine the Mono

The Dark Tower: Roland and his group had a life-threatening riddling contest with this living train.

Black House: Blaine, a monorail in End-World, went crazy and committed suicide.

Oscar (Butch) Bowers

IT: Henry's father caused trouble for neighbors the Hanlons.

Insomnia: He bullied Ralph Roberts in the 1930s.

11/22/63: The family ran BOWERS PRODUCE STAND.

Boyd

Doctor Sleep: a member of 'Round Here

Mr. Mercedes: a member of 'Round Here

Deke Bradford

The Dark Half: a Castle Rock groundskeeper

Needful Things: He submitted a fund-release form requesting $940 for sixteen cases of Taggart Hi-Impact Dynamite to blast away a rock obstruction for access to the gravel pit on Town Road #5. Danforth Keeton increased it to $1,400 to cover twenty cases.

Mrs. Brant

The Shining: She demanded to pay her Overlook Hotel bill with American Express, a card the Hotel no longer accepted.

Doctor Sleep: Danny Torrance received her thought about wanting to get into someone's pants.

The Bradley Gang

IT: The outlaw gang was wanted by the FBI.

Gwendy's Final Task: The Bradley Gang was massacred in the 1930s.

Mr. Ted Brautigan

Hearts in Atlantis: Ted escaped from being a Breaker and befriended Bobby Garfield. Bobby's mother led the Low Men in Yellow Coats to Ted for recapture.

Black House: Mr. Brautigan was the Crimson King's Chief Breaker.

The Dark Tower: Ted and the other Breakers helped Roland and the others stop the Breakers from breaking.

Breakers

Hearts in Atlantis: People with natural abilities the Crimson King forced to break the Dark Tower's Beams

Black House: Telekinetics were the most rare and valuable Breakers.

The Dark Tower: A substance in twins' brains was brain-food for Breakers.

Sheila Brigham

The Dark Half: the Castle County Sheriff's office dispatcher

Needful Things: Sheila killed Lester Pratt when Lester tried to kill Deputy John LaPointe.

Gwendy's Magic Feather: long-time dispatcher at the Castle Rock Sheriff's Department

Gwendy's Final Task: Sheila and her husband, Dusty, retired to Florida.

David Bright

The Dead Zone: Bangor *Daily News* reporter David Bright wrote fair and impartial articles on Johnny Smith.

The Tommyknockers: David wrote about the disappearance of Troopers Peter Gabbons and Benton Rhodes.

Matthew Burke

'Salem's Lot: Matt told Ben Mears he suspected Jerusalem's Lot had a vampire.

The Dark Tower: a teacher in Jerusalem's Lot

Jessie Angela Burlingame

Gerald's Game: Jessie was handcuffed to a bed in her summer home during the off-season.

Dolores Claiborne: Dolores Claiborne knew a woman was in trouble. The woman was the same girl—Jessie Mahout—she had seen during the eclipse, but was all grown up.

Father Donald Callahan

'Salem's Lot: The Father left Jerusalem's Lot after losing his faith battling Kurt Barlow.

The Dark Tower: Pere Callahan hooked up with Roland's ka-tet.

the Cambers: Brett, Charity, and Joe

Cujo: The family lived on Seven Oaks Farm at the end of Town Road #3. A rabid bat bit Brett's lovable dog, Cujo, who went on to kill three people and was responsible for the death of a fourth. Joe and Cujo remained the talk of the town for over a decade.

"The Body": Dumpkeeper Milo Pressman's dog, Chopper, was the most feared dog until Joe Camber's Cujo twenty years later.

"Mrs. Todd's Shortcut": Joe Camber's dog killed him.

"Gramma": Joe Camber's hill was a popular sledding site.

"The Sun Dog": Cujo killed Joe.

Needful Things: Reginald Merrill had land near Joe Camber's Seven Oaks Farm and may have owned the farm. Joe's dog killed Joe, his friend, and Sheriff Bannerman. Fortunately, Joe's wife, Charity, and son were out of town and later moved away.

Lily Cavanaugh

The Talisman: Lily starred in about fifty B-movies in the 1950s, 1960s, and 1970s. She received an Academy Award nomination for Best Supporting Actress for her performance in *Blaze*.

Black House: She was Queen of the B's.

Aunt Evvie Chalmers

Cujo: Two years before, Aunt Evvie became Castle Rock's oldest resident when Arnold Heebert died. When Aunt Evvie died at her kitchen table, Vin Marchant became the oldest.

"The Body": She chased away Ace Merrill and Fuzzy Bracowicz when they were beating on Gordie Lachance.

"The Sun Dog": Polly's great-grandmother

Needful Things: Polly's great-aunt

Polly Chalmers

The Dark Half: Polly ran You Sew and Sew. Annie Pangborn worked part time.

"The Sun Dog": Pop Merrill's Emporium Galorium was next door to You Sew and Sew.

Needful Things: She dated Alan Pangborn.

Chris Chambers

"The Body": Chris, Teddy Duchamp, Gordie Lachance, and Vern Tessio found Ray Brower's body.

Needful Things: Ace Merrill had terrorized Chris and his friends.

Misery Chastain

Misery: Misery Chastain was the main character in Paul Sheldon's series of romance novels.

The Dark Tower: Misery Chastain was in the character Stephen King's *Misery* novel.

Christine

Christine: Christine was not your ordinary red-and-white1958 Plymouth Fury. At the end, she rose from the dead and, along with the dead Roland LeBay, took out Sander Galton.

IT: Having an affinity for dead folks, Christine, driven by a dead Belch Huggins, gave Henry Bowers a ride.

[**Easter Egg**] *11/22/63*: Back in time, George Amberson saw a couple of red-and-white 1958 Plymouth Furies. As Roland LeBay was happily motorvating around Libertyville in Christine at those times, I'd have to say these Furies were not Christine.

Dolores Claiborne

Dolores Claiborne: Dolores killed Joe St. George, but she did not kill Vera Donovan.

Storm of the Century: Although unproven, folks suspected she killed her husband, Joe, during an eclipse.

Deputy Andy Clutterbuck

The Dark Half: a Castle County deputy under Sheriff Pangborn

"The Sun Dog": a deputy under Sheriff Pangborn

Needful Things: He and Sheriff Pangborn investigated the Nettie Cobb-Wilma Jerzyck death scene. A couple of years after losing his wife, Andy drove into Castle Lake and drowned.

"It Grows on You": He became a drunkard after his wife died, and he lost his job with the Castle Rock police.

Lisey's Story: He's ba-ack! [Remember, there are other worlds than these.]

"Drunken Fireworks": Andy was chief of the Castle County Police Department.

Melissa Clutterbuck

Needful Things: Andy's wife, Melissa, was killed in one of Leland Gaunt's pranks.

"It Grows on You": Melissa, Andy's wife, was deceased.

Dr. Cody and Father Cody

'Salem's Lot: Dr. James M. Cody helped Ben Mears fight the Jerusalem's Lot vampires.

The Dark Tower: Early dust jackets of *'Salem's Lot* misidentified the doctor as Father Cody.

Mr. Constantine

"The Sun Dog": the pharmacist at LaVerdiere's Super Drug Store in Castle Rock

Needful Things: the pharmacist at LaVerdiere's

Miss Loretta Coogan

'Salem's Lot: Miss Coogan worked at Spencer's Sundries and Pharmacy.

The Dark Tower: Loretta Coogan sold Donald Callahan a bus ticket to New York City.

Castle Rock Cougars

The Dead Zone: a high school football team

Cujo: The Cougars had T-shirts.

"Gramma": Georgie Bruckner had Castle Rock Cougars book covers.

Dorsey Corcoran

IT: His stepfather killed him in the garage and said he fell from a stepladder.

11/22/63: Dicky Macklin killed him with a recoilless hammer.

Eddie Corcoran

IT: IT in the form of the Creature from the Black Lagoon decapitated him.

11/22/63: He disappeared.

Dwight Cramm

Finders Keepers: Bill Hodges recovered Dwight Cramm's stolen Beechcraft KingAir 350 plane.

The Outsider: Holly Gibney had to threaten legal action before Cramm paid his Finders Keepers bill.

Gage William Creed

Pet Sematary: Devastated over the loss of his son, Louis Creed buried Gage in the Micmac burial ground beyond the Pet Sematary.

Insomnia: After Atropos cut Gage's balloon strings for a Random death, a speeding tanker-truck killed him. Atropos took a sneaker.

the Crimson King

Insomnia: Ed Deepneau fell under his influence when Atropos cut his balloon strings.

Hearts in Atlantis: The Crimson King tasked Breakers to break the Dark Tower's Beams.

Black House: Tyler Marshall could have been one of the two most powerful Breakers of all time.

The Dark Tower: The Crimson King was the baddie who wanted to rule the Tower or topple it if he couldn't.

Gwendy's Final Task: With the Crimson King dead, the taheen sought to destroy the Tower.

Cujo

Cujo: Cujo kills four people after a rabid bat bit him.

"The Body": Dumpkeeper Milo Pressman's dog, Chopper, was the most feared dog until Cujo twenty years later.

Pet Sematary: A large St. Bernard killed four people a couple of years before.

"Mrs. Todd's Shortcut": Joe Camber's dog killed Joe.

The Dark Half: A rabid dog killed Sheriff Bannerman.

"The Sun Dog": Cujo killed George Bannerman, Joe Camber, and Gary Pervier.

Needful Things: Cujo killed the Sheriff, Joe, and Gary. Donna Trenton killed Cujo.

The Dark Tower: The character Stephen King wrote about the Saint Bernard.

the Cumberlands

Hearts in Atlantis: They played the dance in the University of Orono's Lengyll Gym.

Revival: Jamie Morton joined the band when they re-united.

Norman Daniels

Rose Madder: Baddie Norman Daniels went after Rose Daniels when she left him. He got his comeuppance.

Desperation: A crazed Norman Daniels killed Anna Stevenson and broke Cynthia Smith's nose.

Rose McClendon Daniels

Rose Madder: Refusing to suffer further abuse, Rose left Norman Daniels.

Desperation: Norman Daniels's wife [Rose] left him.

Patrick Danville

Insomnia: Patrick Danville's death could jeopardize the Tower and all existence. Ralph Roberts and Lois Chasse were enlisted to stop Ed Deepneau from killing a crowd of people, including Patrick.

The Dark Tower: Dandelo imprisoned Patrick. Roland rescued him.

the Dark Father

'Salem's Lot: The Dark Father authorized Kurt Barlow's admittance into Jerusalem's Lot.

"Sometimes They Come Back": The Dark Father helped Jim Norman deal with the dead boys who came back.

the dark man

The Stand: The dark man (Randall Flagg) set up operations in Las Vegas, NV.

The Dark Tower: The dark man was west of Kansas, perhaps Vegas.

Susan Edwina Day

Insomnia: Women's-rights advocate Susan Day spoke and died in Derry.

Rose Madder: Anna Stevenson had a picture of herself with Susan Day.

Ed Deepneau

Insomnia: The Crimson King influenced Ed Deepneau to fly an airplane into the Derry Civic Center, where two thousand people assembled to hear Susan Day speak on behalf of WomanCare. Patrick Danville was the Crimson King's target.

The Dark Tower: Ed Deepneau was the antagonist in the character Stephen King's *Insomnia*.

Rick Dees

The Dead Zone: After Johnny Smith refused his offer to write a psychic column for the tabloid, *Inside View* reporter Rick Dees used the supermarket magazine to discredit Johnny.

"The Night Flier": Rick tracked the Night Flier through several small airports in the eastern United States.

Queen Laura DeLoessian

The Talisman: Jack Sawyer saved the Queen of the Territories.

Black House: Sophie succeeded her as Queen.

George Elmer Denbrough

_IT_: Pennywise killed him near a storm drain on Witcham Street.

_11/22/63_: George's body was found with an arm missing.

William Denbrough

See the Famous Writer Connections chapter.

Dennis

The Eyes of the Dragon: At the end, Dennis and Thomas went after Flagg.

The Dark Tower: Roland saw Dennis and Thomas pursue Flagg.

Horace M. Derwent

The Shining: Horace Derwent owned the Overlook Hotel.

Doctor Sleep: Several years after his death, Derwent haunted Dan Torrance.

Designated Gawkers

Misery: When word got out that police talked with Annie Wilkes about a missing trooper, local people—Designated Gawkers—drove up her driveway for a closer look at her.

The Tommyknockers: A generic term for those who watch after accidents, such as explosions.

Digger

Pet Sematary: American cemetery workers picked up the Digger nickname.

The Talisman: Carlton (Digger) Atwell, an old friend of Smokey Updike's

The Dark Half: Steven (Digger) Holt worked Homeland Cemetery.

Billy Dodd

The Dead Zone: Frank Dodd's father worked for the B&M railroad. Drunk, he was killed between two flatcars while trying to couple them. Frank's father isn't referenced by name.

"Uncle Otto's Truck": Here we learn that Frank's father's name is Billy, and he drove a tow truck.

Frank Dodd and his victims

The Dead Zone: Dubbed the Castle Rock Strangler, Sheriff's Deputy Frank Dodd killed seven women over five years and two sheriffs. People talked about him for fifteen years after he was caught. His victims:

—Alma Frechette, a waitress at The Coffee Pot whom Frank had dated

—Pauline Toothaker, 71

—Cheryl Moody, 14, a junior high student

—Ann Simons, a college student Frank killed while taking a law enforcement course at the University of Colorado

—Carol Dunbarger, 17, a Castle Rock High School student

—Etta Ringgold, a Castle Rock Elementary School teacher

—Mary Kate Hendrasen, 9, a Castle Rock Elementary School student

Cujo: After killing Alma Frechette, Pauline Toothaker, Cheryl Moody, Carol Dunbarger, Etta Ringgold, and Mary Kate Hendrasen, police officer Frank Dodd became Castle Rock's boogeyman.

"Uncle Otto's Truck": Frank Dodd was referred to as "crazy Frank."

IT: Beverly Rogan mentioned the crazy Castle Rock cop who had killed several women in the town.

The Dark Half: Big George Bannerman, the old Sheriff, had an officer who raped and strangled several women.

Needful Things: Frank Dodd, who killed a few women, has not been forgotten.

Gwendy's Magic Feather: Frank Dodd was the Castle Rock Strangler in the early 1970s.

Henrietta Dodd

The Dead Zone: Henrietta, Frank Dodd's mother, knew he was the Castle Rock Strangler.

Cujo: Mentioned only as Frank's mother, she died of a stroke shortly after her son died. Their house became considered haunted.

"Gramma": Henrietta shared a six-party telephone line with the Bruckners.

Steven Bishoff Dubay

IT: John Garton and Dubay threw Adrian Mellon over the Main Street Bridge into the Kenduskeag for being gay. IT killed Adrian.

Dreamcatcher: Three teenagers threw a gay man into the Derry Canal.

Teddy Duchamp

"The Body": Chris Chambers, Gordie Lachance, Vern Tessio, and Teddy found Ray Brower's body.

Needful Things: Ace Merrill had terrorized Teddy and his friends.

Andy Dufresne

"Rita Hayworth and Shawshank Redemption": Andy, innocent of killing his wife, was convicted of her murder and spent almost three decades in Shawshank State Prison.

"Apt Pupil": Banker Dufresne bought some stocks for Kurt Dussander in another name.

Carol Dunbarger

See "Frank Dodd and his victims."

Dinky Earnshaw

"Everything's Eventual": TransCorp hired Dinky Ellery Earnshaw to use his talent to write letters to folks; these letters caused the recipients to die in accidents or suicides.

The Dark Tower: Dinky fled after killing Mr. Sharpton, his handler. They caught him and made him a Breaker.

Elroy

The Talisman: Elroy tried to stop Jack Sawyer from leaving the Oatley Tap.

Black House: Elroy was one of many who had opposed Jack Sawyer.

Captain Farren

The Talisman: The Captain of the Outer Guards gave Jack Sawyer a special Territories coin and showed him the Outpost Road, heading west.

Black House: Captain Farren helped Jack Sawyer get a glimpse of the Queen of the Territories.

Officer Roscoe Fisher

The Dead Zone: A deputy under Sheriff Bannerman, he was Frank Dodd's partner.

Cujo: He found the Trentons' house ransacked after Vic Trenton worried about his wife not answering the phone.

Flagg

The Eyes of the Dragon: King Roland's closest advisor, Flagg betrayed the King.

The Dark Tower: Roland saw Dennis and Thomas pursue Flagg.

Randall Flagg

The Stand: Randall Flagg represented evil in this good-versus-bad epic.

The Dark Tower: The Ageless Stranger, who took many manifestations, told Andrew Quick a friend used to say, "My life for you." Marten Broadcloak identified himself as Flagg and left a note signed with the initials R.F.

Charlie Fortin

The Dark Half: a Castle Rock groundskeeper

Needful Things: the proprietor of the Western Auto on Main Street in Castle Rock

Mr. Flip

'Salem's Lot: Father Callahan's childhood closet boogeyman

The Dark Tower: Pere Callahan's childhood closet boogeyman

Alma Frechette

See "Frank Dodd and his victims."

Homer Gamache

The Dark Half: George Stark beat him to death with Homer's artificial arm and took his truck.

Needful Things: Someone bludgeoned him with his artificial arm and left his body in a ditch near Homeland Cemetery.

Sunlight Gardener

The Talisman: Jack Parker (Jack Sawyer) and Philip Wolf (Wolf) were incarcerated in the Sunlight Gardener Scripture Home for Wayward Boys.

Black House: Sunlight was Osmond in another world.

Bobby Garfield

Hearts in Atlantis: Bobby watched for signs of low men in yellow coats.

The Dark Tower: Ted Brautigan and Bobby were friends.

John Webber Garton

IT: Steven Dubay and Garton threw Adrian Mellon over the Main Street Bridge into the Kenduskeag for being gay. IT killed Adrian.

Dreamcatcher: Three teenagers tossed a gay man into the Derry Canal.

Carol Gerber

Hearts in Atlantis: one of Bobby Garfield's best friends

The Dark Tower: They threatened to harm Bobby Garfield and Carol Gerber to keep Ted Brautigan in line.

Holly Rachel Gibney

Mr. Mercedes: Holly helped retired detective Hodges with computer forensics.

Finders Keepers: Bill Hodges and Holly Gibney ran Finders Keepers, an unofficial Private Investigation firm.

End of Watch: Holly helped Bill with Brady Hartsfield again.

The Outsider: Alec Pelley called in Holly to investigate the Maitlands' trip to Dayton, OH.

"If It Bleeds": Holly dealt with another kind of outsider.

Richie Ginelli

The Dark Tower: Balazar associate Ginelli ran Four Fathers in New York City.

Thinner: Organized crime figure Richie Ginelli was a silent partner in Thee Brothers in New York City.

The Plant: *Mafioso* Richie Ginelli owned Four Fathers in New York City.

Danny Glick

'Salem's Lot: Daniel Francis Glick was one of Barlow's early victims in Jerusalem's Lot.

The Dark Tower: Father Callahan presided over Danny's funeral.

God

The Stand: With Mother Abagail as an intermediary, God sent Glen Bateman, Ralph Brentner, Stu Redman, and Larry Underwood to stand against Randall Flagg. Kojak tagged along.

"The Beggar and the Diamond": To cheer up the saddened Uriel, God helped Ramu.

"An Evening at God's": God smashed Earth because it obstructed His view of His TV.

Dick Hallorann

The Shining: Dick shared shining moments with Danny Torrance.

IT: He helped Will Hanlon, Mike's father, get out of the burning Black Spot, Company E's night club.

Doctor Sleep: He told Danny Torrance how to handle ghosts that have become too real.

Mike Hanlon

IT: One of the Losers, Mike remained in Derry as the others moved away. He called them back.

Insomnia: Head librarian Mike Hanlon gave Helen Deepneau a job after she split from Ed Deepneau.

Dreamcatcher: A plaque on the pedestal where the Derry Standpipe once stood memorialized those lost in the storm of May 31, 1985. The plaque was from the Losers' Club: Ben, Bev, Bill, Eddie, Richie, Stan, and Mike.

Ben Hanscom

IT: Ben and the other Losers fought IT—twice.

Insomnia: Ben designed the New Derry Civic Center in a 1950s style after the old one was destroyed in The Flood of '85.

Dreamcatcher: A plaque on the pedestal where the Derry Standpipe once stood memorialized those lost in the storm of May 31, 1985. The plaque was from the Losers' Club: Bev, Bill, Eddie, Mike, Richie, Stan, and Ben.

11/22/63: Ben told Richie Tozier that Mrs. Dunning had kicked out Mr. Dunning.

Brady Wilson Hartsfield

Mr. Mercedes: Brady Hartsfield was the Mercedes Killer.

Finders Keepers: Brady lay in a coma in Room 217 of the Traumatic Brain Injury Clinic at Kiner Memorial Hospital.

End of Watch: Brady woke from his coma and found terrifying ways to use Zappit game consoles.

The Outsider: The deceased Brady was a horrible person Holly Gibney had dealt with.

"If It Bleeds": Holly reminisced about the evil of Brady Hartsfield.

Mary Kate Hendrasen

See "Frank Dodd and his victims."

Naomi Sarah Higgins

"The Library Policeman": She helped Sam Peebles deal with Ardelia Lortz.

Needful Things: She married Sam Peebles. They moved away.

Kermit William Hodges

Mr. Mercedes: Retired detective Hodges met Brady Hartsfield.

Finders Keepers: Bill Hodges and Holly Gibney ran Finders Keepers, an unofficial Private Investigation firm.

End of Watch: Bill tussles with Brady Hartsfield again.

The Outsider: Alec Pelley had gotten Bill the Oliver Madden/Dwight Cramm gig.

"If It Bleeds": The late Bill Hodges was Holly's mentor in work and life.

Patrick Hockstetter

IT: Flying leeches from IT attacked Patrick at the dump. IT carried him to the Derry sewer system, where he died of blood loss.

11/22/63: His decayed body was found in the Barrens.

Charlie Hogan

"The Body": To become famous in Castle Rock, Ace Merrill, Charlie, and others went to discover Ray Brower's body. Gordie

Lachance and friends sent them away. Nobody took credit for the discovery; Ace made an anonymous phone call.

"Nona": Charlie told Ace Merrill that the narrator was getting friendly with Betsy Malenfant, Ace's girlfriend.

Hollis

"Nona": The narrator was a ward of the state, living with the Hollises. Nona led him to a cemetery, where he was found next to the graves of his parents and brothers. He was sent to jail or a mental institution.

Gerald's Game: *Castonguay vs. Hollis* was cited during Raymond Andrew Joubert's arraignment. For several years, Joubert had been desecrating graveyards in western Maine.

Hollywood Girls

Joyland: Each Happy Helper team had an attractive Hollywood Girl in a short green dress to take pictures of guests, and then offered to sell prints as souvenirs.

Revival: Hollywood Girls took pictures of Joyland park patrons.

Detective John (Jack) P. Hoskins

The Outsider: The outsider tricked Hoskins into keeping him safe at the Marysville Hole.

"If It Bleeds": Detective Hoskins was killed in the outsider case.

Pete Huntley

Mr. Mercedes: Bill Hodges and Pete Huntley's initial investigation of the Mercedes Killer led nowhere.

Finders Keepers: Bill Hodges gave Pete Huntley the Oliver Madden collar.

End of Watch: Holly Gibney brought retired detective Pete Huntley on board at Finders Keepers after Bill Hodges died.

The Outsider: Pete continued working with Holly Gibney at Finders Keepers.

"If It Bleeds": While Holly dealt with a new type of outsider, Pete took care of other business.

Island Princess

Dolores Claiborne: The *Island Princess* ferry ran between Little Tall and the mainland.

"Home Delivery": The *Island Princess* served Jenny and Little Tall Islands.

Sonny Jackett

The Dark Half: ran Sonny's Sunoco in Castle Rock

"The Sun Dog": ran Sonny's Texaco in Castle Rock

Needful Things: ran Sonny's Sunoco in Castle Rock

Isabelle Jaynes

Mr. Mercedes: Izzy Jaynes became Pete Huntley's partner after Bill Hodges retired.

Finders Keepers: Detective Jaynes was Pete Huntley's partner.

End of Watch: She and Detective Huntley investigated the Stover-Ellerton murder-suicide.

The Outsider: Holly Gibney didn't like Izzy Jaynes, Pete Huntley's old partner.

Raymond Andrew Joubert

Gerald's Game: Joubert had been a perpetual graveyard desecrater, doing creepy things with corpses.

Insomnia: Ed Deepneau thought John Tandy had aborted baby parts in the back of his trucks. After Tandy showed his fertilizer barrels contained no babies, Ed proclaimed that John wasn't Dahmer or Ray Joubert after all.

Eddie Kaspbrak

IT: Eddie and the Losers (not a rock band) fought IT.

Dreamcatcher: A plaque on the pedestal where the Derry Standpipe once stood memorialized those lost in the storm of May 31, 1985. The plaque was from the Losers' Club: Ben, Bev, Bill, Mike, Richie, Stan, and Eddie.

Norbert Keene

IT: He ran the Center Street Drug Store in Derry.

11/22/63: George Amberson didn't like him.

Bill Keeton

The Dark Half: He was referred to only as Danforth Keeton's uncle, who was buried in the family plot at Homeland Cemetery.

Needful Things: He died in Juniper Hill.

Danforth (Buster) Keeton

The Dark Half: George Stark was buried in one of his unused family plots at Homeland Cemetery.

"The Sun Dog": Mr.Keeton worked in the Castle Rock selectman's office.

Needful Things: He was one of Leland Gaunt's best pranksters.

Gert Kinshaw

Rose Madder: Gert Kinshaw stopped Norman Daniels from biting on Cynthia Smith and peed on him.

Desperation: Gert was Cynthia Smith's friend.

Cam Knowles

Doctor Sleep: a member of 'Round Here

Mr. Mercedes: the lead singer of 'Round Here

End of Watch: Jamie Winters had a special feeling for 'Round Here's Cam Knowles.

Gordon Lachance

See the Famous Writer Connections chapter.

Deputy John LaPointe

The Dark Half: Castle County's number-two deputy under Sheriff Pangborn

Needful Things: Lester Pratt broke his nose and continued pounding on him. Sheila Brigham saved him by killing Pratt.

Gerald's Game: He and Sheriff Ridgewick caught Raymond Andrew Joubert while staking out Homeland Cemetery.

Mike Latimer

"The Crate": The creature from the crate killed him.

Christine: Horlicks University had a job opening for a janitor that had disappeared.

Lemkes

Thinner: Many Lemkes traveled with Taduz Lemke's band of Gypsies.

11/22/63: Jake Epping taught about twenty-four Lemkes in just a few years of teaching.

the Library Police

"The Library Policeman": They went after those who didn't return their library books. Sometimes, they got nasty.

Hearts in Atlantis: Ted Brautigan wasn't a bad guy. At most, the Library Police would be after him if they existed.

"Morality": Nora Callahan called Officer Abromowitz a library policeman when he informed her she had four overdue books.

the Little Sisters

The Dark Tower: A traveling *ka-tet* of vampires.

Black House: Their last tent stood in the borderland between the Territories and Mid-World.

Lloyd

The Shining: He served Jack Torrance in the Colorado Lounge while the Overlook Hotel was closed—and dry—for the winter.

Doctor Sleep: the bartender at the Overlook Hotel

The Losers' Club

IT: The Losers—Bill Denbrough, Mike Hanlon, Ben Hanscom, Eddie Kaspbrak, Bev Marsh, Richie Tozier, and Stan Uris—fought IT.

Dreamcatcher: The Losers' Club—Bill, Ben, Bev, Eddie, Richie, Stan, and Mike—dedicated a plaque to those lost in the big storm.

low men in yellow coats

The Dark Tower: Also known as can-toi, they are creatures with rat faces who wore human masks and dressed in mustard-colored trench coats over flashy clothing. They served the Crimson King.

Hearts in Atlantis: Low men caught Ted Brautigan after he escaped again.

"Ur": Two low men warned Wesley Smith to not mess with the timeline again.

Gwendy's Final Task: Creatures consistent with low men killed Gwendy's husband, Ryan Brown.

Richard P. Macklin

IT: Richard Macklin killed Dorsey Corcoran and said the boy fell in the garage.

11/22/63: Dicky Macklin killed Dorsey with a recoilless hammer.

Oliver Madden

Finders Keepers: Oliver Madden used the alias James Mallon to con Dwight Cramm.

The Outsider: Bill Hodges recovered Dwight Cramm's stolen airplane from Oliver Madden.

Jessie Angela Mahout

Gerald's Game: While cleaning up after an inappropriate incident on her father's lap during the eclipse, she saw a country woman kneeling over boards and peering into a well.

Dolores Claiborne: When the eclipse started, Dolores St. George saw a little girl sitting on her father's lap and watching the eclipse; he had his hand too high on her thigh. Later, after she had caused her husband to fall into a well, she saw the girl, looking under a bed miles away, turn and look at her.

Beverly Marsh

IT: Beverly and the Losers (not a rock band) fought IT. When they fought IT in the sewers beneath Derry as children, Beverly had a neat trick to help them find their way out.

Dreamcatcher: A plaque on the pedestal where the Derry Standpipe once stood memorialized those lost in the storm of May 31, 1985. The plaque was from the Losers' Club: Ben, Bill, Eddie, Mike, Richie, Stan, and Bev.

11/22/63: George Amberson saw Bev and Richie Tozier learning to swing-dance to the Glenn Miller Orchestra.

Dorrance Marstellar

Revival: In the 1960s, Dorrance had a cornfield near the First Methodist Church of Harlow.

"Mr. Harrigan's Phone": In the early 2000s he kept hens in his barn.

[**Easter Egg**] *Insomnia*: In the early 1990s, Dor was one of Derry's Harris Avenue Old Crocks.

Mrs. Massey

The Shining: She overdosed and died in the bathtub of Room 217 at the Overlook Hotel. Four months later, she half-strangled Danny Torrance.

Doctor Sleep: Several years later, she found Danny Torrance in Florida. Dick Hallorann told how to deal with her.

Charlene (Charlie) Norma Roberta McGee

Firestarter: The Shop wanted her power.

The Tommyknockers: The Shop had rebuilt their Virginia compound, which a child had destroyed. Note: Charlie is not named.

Adrian Mellon

IT: Steven Dubay and John Garton threw Adrian over the Main Street Bridge into the Kenduskeag for being gay. IT killed Adrian.

Insomnia: A little after the Derry, ME, Canal Days Festival, three boys threw him over the bridge into the Kenduskeag River behind the Falcon Tavern because they didn't like his hat. He had been bitten and stabbed to death.

Dreamcatcher: Three teenagers dropped a gay man into the Derry Canal.

Ace Merrill

"The Body": To become famous in Castle Rock, Ace Merrill and a carload of friends went to discover Ray Brower's body. Gordie Lachance and his pals sent them away. Nobody took credit for the discovery; Ace made an anonymous phone call.

"Nona": Ace beat up the narrator for getting too chummy with Betsy Malenfant, Ace's girlfriend.

"The Sun Dog": Ace served four years in Shawshank for breaking and entering The Mellow Tiger.

Needful Things: He and Buster Keeton planted explosives throughout town.

Reginald (Pop) Merrill

"The Sun Dog": Pop Merrill helped Kevin Delevan with a strange Polaroid camera. His effort killed him.

Needful Things: Ace Merrill inherited only the $4,000 he had in the bank. Pop's fortune was never found.

Cheryl Moody

See "Frank Dodd and his victims."

Jim Morrison

The Stand: Years after he supposedly died, Jim Morrison pulled up for gas during Stu Redman's shift at Hapscomb's Texaco.

"You Know They Got a Hell of a Band": Jim Morrison lived in Rock and Roll Heaven, OR, after he died.

Aloysious Nell

IT: This Derry police officer found the Losers had built a dam that created a serious backup in Derry. He let them off easy by explaining the nuisance and telling them to dismantle their dam.

Insomnia: a past Derry, ME, police officer and Officer Chris Nell's grandfather

Chris Nell

Insomnia: He and Detective Leydecker arrested Ed Deepneau for assaulting Helen Deepneau.

Dreamcatcher: Officer Nell patrolled Derry.

Don Nell

[**Easter Egg**] "Sometimes They Come Back": a retired Stratford, CT, police officer

The Night Flier / Popsy

"Popsy": a vampire his grandson called "Popsy"

"The Night Flier": Rick Dees of *Inside View* dubbed a vampire "The Night Flier." Stephen King identified him as the same guy as Popsy.

Elevation: *Inside View* featured the Night Flier.

"If It Bleeds": *Inside View* ran Night Flier stories for a year.

Niner

The Eyes of the Dragon: King Roland slew the dragon Niner.

The Dark Tower: Niner was not named but referenced as the last dragon in the area around Garlan. A king that was later murdered had slain it.

Virginia Norey

Virginia Norey revised a Maine eclipse-coverage map to show places from *Sky and Telescope* magazine. The map had been adapted from a Department of Economic Development map.

Gerald's Game showed the map.

Dolores Claiborne also showed the map.

Susan Norton

'Salem's Lot: Ben Mears drove a stake through her Undead heart.

The Dark Tower: Barlow turned her into a Type Two vampire.

Odell

Mr. Mercedes: Odell was the Robinsons' Irish Setter.

Finders Keepers: Jerome Robinson brought Odell with him to visit Bill Hodges.

End of Watch: Brady Hartsfield's mother had died from the poison Brady meant for Odell.

"If It Bleeds": Odell died of congestive heart failure.

Osmond

The Talisman: He suffocated Jason DeLoessian.

Black House: Sunlight Gardener's counterpart in another world

the outsider

The Outsider: The outsider fed on children and left irrefutable evidence implicating others for his crimes.

"If It Bleeds": Not long after defeating the outsider, Holly Gibney dealt with another type of outsider.

Sheriff Alan J. Pangborn

The Dark Half: The Castle County Sheriff, he eventually believed Thad Beaumont's outrageous idea that Thad's pseudonym and come to life and went on a murderous rampage.

"The Sun Dog": He arrested Ace Merrill for breaking into The Mellow Tiger.

Needful Things: He cast Leland Gaunt out of Castle Rock.

Gerald's Game: Norris Ridgewick succeeded Alan as Castle County Sheriff.

Bag of Bones: He and Polly moved to New Hampshire.

Gwendy's Magic Feather: Norris Ridgewick succeeded Alan as Castle County Sheriff.

Annie Pangborn

The Dark Half: Alan's wife worked part time for Polly Chalmers.

Needful Things: A brain tumor was instrumental in the accident that caused her and Todd Pangborn's deaths.

Todd Pangborn

The Dark Half: Annie and Alan Pangborn's son

Needful Things: On the way to Hemphill's Market, his mother struck a tree at 70+ MPH. Both were killed.

Speedy Parker

The Talisman: Speedy was in the right place at the right time to get Jack Sawyer started as Travelin' Jack.

Black House: Speedy helped Jack Sawyer once more.

Parkus

The Talisman: A lawman in the Territories, he was Speedy Parker in our world.

Black House: Parkus explained what the Crimson King was up to with Breakers.

Patricia

The Dark Tower: This monorail train drowned herself in the Send River.

Black House: Patricia, a monorail in End-World, went crazy and committed suicide.

Lenny Partridge

Needful Things: Castle Rock's oldest resident

Mr. Mercedes: a member of 'Round Here

Franklin Victor Peterson

The Outsider: Appearing as Terry Maitland, the outsider killed Frankie Peterson.

"If It Bleeds": The outsider brutally murdered Frank Peterson.

Mark Petrie

'Salem's Lot: He helped Ben Mears defeat Barlow.

The Dark Tower: Mark attended Ben Mears's funeral in Los Zapatos, Mexico.

Dave Phillips

The Dark Half: the Beaumonts' summer-home caretaker

Needful Things: a Castle Rock handyman and caretaker available for private hire

Upson Pratt

"They're Creeping Up on You" from *Creepshow*: Roaches overran his apartment and overwhelmed him.

Creepshow 2: An advertisement in an issue of *Creepshow* had a drawing of a man resembling Upson Pratt.

Norris Ridgewick

The Dark Half: Deputy Ridgewick was a George Stark fan.

"The Sun Dog": a Castle Rock deputy

Needful Things: Ace Merill shot him. He returned the favor by killing Ace.

Gerald's Game: Sheriff Ridgewick and Deputy LaPointe caught Raymond Andrew Joubert while staking out Homeland Cemetery.

Bag of Bones: Investigating the whereabouts of Kyra Devore, he arrived at Mike Noonan's summer home and found her safe and sound.

Lisey's Story: Sheriff Ridgewick and his wife honeymooned on Maui.

Gwendy's Magic Feather: Sheriff Ridgewick kept Gwendy Peterson in the loop about the investigation of missing young girls.

Gwendy's Final Task: Norris retired after almost twenty years as Sheriff.

Etta Ringgold

See "Frank Dodd and his victims."

Lois Roberts

Insomnia: Lois helped Ralph Roberts return after saving Patrick Danville.

Bag of Bones: She was a Red Cross volunteer.

Ralph Roberts

Insomnia: Ralph Roberts saved Patrick Danville.

Bag of Bones: He suggested Mike Noonan take a vacation.

The Dark Tower: Ralph stopped the worst from happening re Ed Deepneau.

Barbara Rosellen Robinson

Mr. Mercedes: Barb went to the 'Round Here concert at Mingo Auditorium. So did Brady Hartsfield.

Finders Keepers: Barbara went to Chapel Ridge, a private school.

End of Watch: Brady Hartsfield used a Zappit to mess with her head.

"If It Bleeds": Chet Ondowsky took Barb when she and Jerome went to Finders Keepers to check on Holly Gibney.

Jerome Peter Robinson

Mr. Mercedes: Bill Hodges's all-around handy guy helped Holly Gibney and Bill defeat Brady Hartsfield at Mingo Auditorium.

Finders Keepers: Jerome helped Holly and Bill deal with Morris Bellamy.

End of Watch: Jerome played a key role in putting Brady Hartsfield to rest.

The Outsider: Holly's friend Jerome vacationed in Ireland.

"If It Bleeds": Jerome took another year off from his career of going to school to write a book on how his great-great-grandfather became a successful gangster.

Tanya Robinson

Mr. Mercedes: Mrs. Robinson took Barbara and friends to the 'Round Here concert at Mingo Auditorium.

Finders Keepers: She, Barb, and Tina Saubers made popcorn balls.

End of Watch: She and Mr. Robinson brought Barbara home from the hospital.

"If It Bleeds": She cooked Thanksgiving dinner and invited Holly Gibney.

Roland

aka: Roland Deschain, Roland of Gilead

Insomnia: a gunfighter in a Patrick Danville drawing

Black House: The last of his kind, he devoted his life to protecting the Beams and the Tower.

The Dark Tower: Others join Roland in his quest for The Dark Tower.

King Roland

The Eyes of the Dragon: King Roland slew the dragon Niner. Later, Flagg poisoned the King.

The Dark Tower: King Roland was not named but referenced as a king who killed the last dragon in the area around Garlan and was later murdered.

'Round Here

Doctor Sleep: a boy band popular with teenage girls

Mr. Mercedes: Holly Gibney stopped Brady Hartsfield from executing a terrorist plot at the 'Round Here concert.

Finders Keepers: They were to perform in Barbara Robinson's city.

End of Watch: Barbara Robinson and friends accepted free Zappit Commanders as consolation for the ruined 'Round Here concert.

"If It Bleeds": Holly, Bill Hodges, and Jerome Robinson saved thousands of kids at the 'Round Here concert in the Midwest Culture and Arts Complex.

Rusty

The Dead Zone: Old and blind, George Bannerman's Irish Setter didn't have much time left.

Cujo: Rusty had to be put down in 1976.

Jack Sawyer

The Talisman: Master Sawyer became Travelin Jack to save his mother and her Twinner.

Black House: Jack thwarted the Crimson King's acquisition of one of the two best Breakers of all time.

Lily Sawyer

The Talisman: Jack retrieved the Talisman to save her.

Black House: She died a few years later.

Phil Sawyer

The Talisman: He introduced business partner Morgan Sloat to the Territories. Big mistake; Sloat had him killed.

Black House: His wife sold his half of Sawyer & Sloat to set herself and her son up for life.

Mr. Sharpton

"Everything's Eventual": Mr. Sharpton gave Dinky Earnshaw a job with awesome benefits.

The Dark Tower: Dinky Earnshaw killed Mr. Sharpton and fled. They caught him and made him a Breaker.

Paul Sheldon

See the Famous Writer Connections chapter.

Julia Shumway

"N.": Julia Shumway wrote an article for the Chester's Mill *Democrat*.

Under the Dome: Julia Shumway ran the *Democrat* and helped Dale Barbara.

Ann Simons

See "Frank Dodd and his victims."

Henry Sirois

Mr. Mercedes: Henry flew in for Edith Wharton's funeral.

End of Watch: Henry was Holly Gibney's uncle.

"If It Bleeds": Charlotte Gibney and Holly Gibney took Uncle Henry to the Rolling Hills Elder Care Center.

Morgan of Orris

The Talisman: Morgan Sloat's Twinner

Black House: He raped and hurt Sophie such that she couldn't bear children.

Morgan Sloat

The Talisman: He died trying to stop Jack Sawyer from reaching the Talisman.

Black House: Lily Sawyer stopped his embezzling from Sawyer & Sloat.

Richard Sloat

The Talisman: Jack Sawyer's best friend

Black House: He grew up to run a law firm.

slow mutants

The Dark Tower: mutated humanoid creatures that appeared to be suffering radiation sickness

Black House: They also inhabited the Blasted Lands in the Territories.

Cynthia Smith

Rose Madder: Cynthia joined Daughters and Sisters after her boyfriend had nearly torn off her left ear.

Desperation: Cynthia became a counselor at D&S.

Note: Although she has a similar description, the Cynthia Smith in *The Regulators* is not this Cynthia Smith. See the Appendix "Desperation / The Regulators Character Comparison."

Johnny Smith

The Dead Zone: Johnny identified the Castle Rock Strangler and stopped Greg Stillson's political career from escalating to the point of starting a nuclear war.

Cujo: John Smith exposed Frank Dodd as a killer.

The Tommyknockers: David Bright had written an article about Johnny, a psychic teacher who had tried to assassinate Stillson.

Needful Things: He knew the identity of a killer when he stood on Castle Rock's Town Common's bandstand.

the Speaking Demon

The Dark Tower: The Speaking Demon told Roland that Jake would hinder his quest.

Black House: In a circle of stones abandoned by the Speaking Demon, Parkus brought Jack Sawyer up to date with the Crimson King's plans to use Breakers to take down the Beams holding the Dark Tower.

Springheel Jack

"Strawberry Spring": Every Strawberry Spring, he killed female New Sharon Teachers' College students at night. He was never caught.

"Apt Pupil": Kurt Dussander remarked that the media loves reporting about serial killers, such as the Wino Killer (the team of Todd Bowden and Dussander), Springheel Jack, and others.

Dolores Claiborne St. George

Gerald's Game: While cleaning up after an inappropriate incident on her father's lap during the eclipse, Jessie Mahout saw a country woman kneeling over boards and peering into a well.

Dolores Claiborne: When the eclipse started, Dolores saw a little girl sitting on her father's lap and watching the eclipse; he had his hand too high on her thigh. Later, after she had caused her husband to fall into a well, she saw the girl, looking under a bed miles away, turn and look at her.

Joe St. George

Dolores Claiborne: Dolores St. George killed the abusive Joe.

Storm of the Century: Although unproven, folks suspected Dolores Claiborne killed Joe in an eclipse.

Selena St. George

Dolores Claiborne: Dolores killed Joe St. George to make sure he never molested Selena again.

"Home Delivery": Selena came back to Little Tall once for Thanksgiving, then never returned.

Starbirds

Thinner: Starbirds traveled with Taduz Lemke's band of Gypsies.

Bag of Bones: The southern Castle County phone book listed many Starbirds.

11/22/63: Jake Epping taught about twenty-four Starbirds in just a few years of teaching.

George Stark

See the Famous Writer Connections chapter.

Steve

Doctor Sleep: a member of 'Round Here

Mr. Mercedes: a member of 'Round Here

Anna Stevenson

Rose Madder: Anna Stevenson ran Daughters and Sisters. Norm Daniels got her.

Desperation: Norman Daniels killed her.

Greg Ammas Stillson

The Dead Zone: Johnny Smith stopped Stillson's political career from escalating to the point of starting a nuclear war.

The Tommyknockers: David Bright had written an article about Johnny, a psychic teacher who had tried to assassinate Stillson, a New Hampshire Congressman.

The Dark Tower: Greg Stillson appeared in the character Stephen King's *The Dead Zone*.

Richard Straker

'Salem's Lot: Straker paved the way for Barlow's presence in Jerusalem's Lot.

The Dark Tower: Mark Petrie killed Straker.

John L. Sullivan (Sully-John)

Hearts in Atlantis: John Sullivan grew up in Harwich, CT, survived the Vietnam War, and died of a heart attack.

The Dark Tower: Sully-John was Bobby Garfield's friend.

taheen

The Dark Tower: Human-like creatures with the heads of animals provided security at Devor-Toi, the compound that housed the Breakers.

Gwendy's Final Task: With the Crimson King dead, the taheen sought Gwendy's button box to destroy the Tower with the black button.

Vern Tessio

"The Body": Chris Chambers, Gordie Lachance, Teddy Duchamp, and Vern found Ray Brower's body.

"Nona": Vern flunked out of school.

Needful Things: Ace Merrill had terrorized Vern and his friends.

Thomas

The Eyes of the Dragon: At the end, Dennis and Thomas went after Flagg

The Dark Tower: Roland saw Dennis and Thomas pursue Flagg.

Seaton Thomas

The Dark Half: a Castle County deputy under Sheriff Pangborn

Needful Things: He found Nettie Cobb and Wilma Jerzyck dead after a report of two women fighting with knives.

Pauline Toothaker

See “Frank Dodd and his victims.”

Tony

The Shining: Danny Torrance’s invisible friend warned Danny of danger.

Doctor Sleep: Tony became active again. Abra Stone reached out.

Brett Torrance

The Shining: Jack Torrance’s brother died fighting in Vietnam’s Dong Ho province.

Doctor Sleep: Danny Torrance’s uncle

Daniel (Danny) Anthony Torrance

The Shining: The Overlook Hotel wanted Danny.

Storm of the Century: Danny didn’t appear as a character, but the text mentioned that he liked *The Little Puppy*.

Doctor Sleep: Danny helped Abra Stone defeat the True Knot.

John (Jack) Daniel Torrance

The Shining: The Overlook Hotel wanted Danny Torrance and enlisted Jack to get him.

Misery: When talking about Andrew Pomeroy, Annie Wilkes mentioned that the Overlook Hotel's crazy caretaker had burned it down ten years before.

The Dark Tower: The character Stephen King wrote about the haunted father Jack in *The Shining*.

Doctor Sleep: Alcoholic Dan Torrance's father was an alcoholic.

Mark Anthony Torrance

The Shining: Jack Torrance's father

Doctor Sleep: He nearly beat his wife to death.

Mike Torrance

The Shining: Jack Torrance's brother

Doctor Sleep: Dan Torrance's uncle

Wendy Torrance

The Shining: Wendy survived the Overlook Hotel.

Doctor Sleep: She died from smoking.

Richie Tozier

IT: Richie and the Losers defeated IT the second time they fought IT.

Dreamcatcher: A plaque on the pedestal where the Derry Standpipe once stood memorialized those lost in the storm of May 31, 1985. The plaque was from the Losers' Club: Ben, Bev, Bill, Eddie, Mike, Stan, and Richie.

The Girl Who Loved Tom Gordon: Richie "Records" Tozier wrote the lyrics to "Gotta Get Next to You (Jus' Slip Me a Taste)," performed by Boyz To Da Maxx.

Duma Key: R. Tozier and W. Denbrough wrote the lyrics to "Dig," performed by Shark Puppy.

11/22/63: George Amberson saw Beverly Marsh and Richie learning to swing-dance to the Glenn Miller Orchestra.

Phil Tracker

IT: Phil and his brother, Tony, owned and operated The Tracker Brothers' Truck Depot. It went out of business before 1985.

Dreamcatcher: Beaver, Henry Devlin, Jonesy, and Pete Moore met Duddits outside the Tracker Brothers' abandoned depot.

11/22/63: The Trackers had a family mausoleum at Longview Cemetery in Derry.

Tony Tracker

IT: Tony and his brother, Phil, owned and operated The Tracker Brothers' Truck Depot.

Dreamcatcher: Beaver, Henry Devlin, Jonesy, and Pete Moore met Duddits outside the Tracker Brothers' abandoned depot.

11/22/63: The Trackers had a family mausoleum at Longview Cemetery in Derry.

The Trashcan Man

The Stand: The Trashcan Man served Randall Flagg.

The Dark Tower: The Ageless Stranger told Andrew Quick a friend used to say, "My life for you."

Donna and Tad Trenton

Cujo: Donna Trenton's Ford Pinto stalled often. She took it to Camber's Garage, but the place was deserted except for Cujo, who kept her and her son, Tad, trapped in the car for a couple of days.

"The Sun Dog": Cujo trapped a woman and her son in their car for two or three days. The boy died.

Needful Things: Cujo killed Tad on Joe Camber's farm. Donna killed the dog with a baseball bat.

the True Knot

Doctor Sleep: Tragic events tended to release much steam. The True Knot fed on steam and traveled in RVs.

"If It Bleeds": Holly Gibney noticed a Winnebago in the background of news coverage reporting the bomb blast at Albert Macready Middle School.

Smokey Updike

The Talisman: Jack Sawyer provided him with cheap labor at the Oatley Tap . . .

Black House: . . . and he wouldn't let Jack leave.

Chris Philip Unwin

IT: Chris held Don Hagarty as Steve Dubay and John Garton tossed Adrian Mellon into the Kenduskeag for being gay.

Dreamcatcher: Three teenagers threw a gay man into the Derry Canal.

Stan Uris

IT: Sadly, Stan only fought IT once. The other Losers fought IT twice.

Dreamcatcher: A plaque on the pedestal where the Derry Standpipe once stood memorialized those lost in the storm of May 31, 1985. The plaque was from the Losers' Club: Ben, Bev, Bill, Eddie, Mike, Richie, and Stan.

Dr. Ray Van Allen

The Dark Half: Castle County medical examiner and coroner

Needful Things: Henry Beaufort died en route to the hospital after being shot. Dr. Van Allen found an unknown, deadly poison on the bullet.

Jordy Verrill

"Weeds"/"The Lonesome Death of Jordy Verrill": Jordy was the unfortunate victim of a fast-growing weed he let loose when he broke a meteorite by pouring water on it.

"Old Chief Wood'nhead": Steve Gribbens bought a TV from Jordy Verrill's junkyard.

walk-ins

The Institute: WMDK talk-show host George Allman discussed walk-ins. A walk-in was a human possessed by a demon; when the demon was done with that person, it walked back out and left only a shell.

Later: Mr. Burkett called the demon infesting Ken Therriault a walk-in and warned that it was very dangerous.

[**Easter Egg**] In *The Dark Tower*, walk-ins were people who suddenly appeared in the Keystone World. Stephen King's property at #19 Turtleback Lane in Lovell, ME, was ground zero.

Harvey Watson

The Shining: Watson showed Jack Torrance what he had to do as The Overlook Hotel's winter caretaker.

Doctor Sleep: Watson was The Overlook Hotel's caretaker.

Elizabeth Sirois Wharton

Mr. Mercedes: She gave retired Detective Bill Hodges a new insight into Olivia Trelawney's suicide.

End of Watch: Elizabeth was Olivia Trelawney's mother. [Here, she is named only Elizabeth.]

"If It Bleeds": Holly Gibney had a familial resemblance to Aunt Elizabeth. [This story refers to Aunt Elizabeth without a last name.]

Annie Wilkes

Misery: Anne Marie Wilkes was Paul Sheldon's Number One Fan, and she proved it.

The Dark Tower: The character Stephen King wrote about Annie Wilkes in *Misery*.

Wolf

The Talisman: Wolf died protecting his herd—Jack Sawyer.

Black House: Jack Sawyer's friend in the past.

Joe Wyzer

Insomnia: pharmacist at the Rite Aid across from Derry, ME's Strawford Park

Bag of Bones: He transferred to a Bangor Rite Aid.

Famous Writer Connections

There are other writers than these, Gwendy Peterson, for example. Included here are only those who are well known and establish connections. An appendix shows an exhaustive collection of writers among Stephen King's characters.

Roberta Anderson

The Tommyknockers: Best-selling author Roberta Anderson discovered a spaceship buried on her property.

The Stand: An author in Haven wrote a Western called *Rimfire Christmas*. Fran Goldsmith read four chapters to the dying Gus Dinsmore.

Thaddeus Beaumont

The Dark Half: Thad wrote under his own name and with the George Stark pseudonym.

Needful Things: Thad's wife and twins left him after he became a drunk.

Bag of Bones: He committed suicide.

William Denbrough

IT: Loser Bill Denbrough grew up to become a successful horror novelist.

Bag of Bones: Jo Noonan was a fan.

Dreamcatcher: A plaque on the pedestal where the Derry Standpipe once stood memorialized those lost in the storm of May 31, 1985. The plaque was from the Losers' Club: Ben, Bev, Eddie, Mike, Richie, Stan, and Bill.

Duma Key: R. Tozier and W. Denbrough wrote the lyrics to "Dig," performed by Shark Puppy.

Stephen King

The Dark Tower: Stephen King's writing the Dark Tower story was responsible for preserving all existence.

"The Rock and Roll Dead Zone": The Gooch pitched an idea about a rock and roll death-oriented theme park to Steve.

"Blockade Billy": George Grantham told Mr. King about the season Billy Blakely played for the New Jersey Titans.

Gordon Lachance

"The Body": Young teen Gordie wrote stories, such as "The Revenge of Lard Ass Hogan" and "Stud City."

Needful Things: Gordie had moved away and become a big-shot writer.

Ben Mears

'Salem's Lot: Ben returned to Jerusalem's Lot to write about the Marsten House.

The Dark Tower: Donald Callahan went todash to attend Ben's funeral in Los Zapatos, Mexico.

Michael Noonan

Bag of Bones: Mike retired from writing.

Lisey's Story: Darla Debusher listened to Michael Noonan audio books.

Paul Sheldon

Misery: Paul wrote a series of romance novels featuring Misery Chastain.

"The Library Policeman": a romance novelist

Rose Madder: Norm Daniels beat up Rosie, his four-month-pregnant wife, for reading *Misery's Journey*. Rosie had a miscarriage.

Desperation: Paul isn't mentioned, but Ellen Carver read *Misery in Paradise*.

The Dark Tower: The character Stephen King wrote about Paul Sheldon in *Misery*.

George Stark

The Dark Half: Thad Beaumont wrote his darker material under the George Stark pseudonym.

Needful Things: He drove a Toronado.

Bag of Bones: Stark's *Steel Machine* appeared ahead of Mike Noonan's *The Red-Shirt Man* on *The New York Times* best-seller list.

Miscellaneous Connections

can tahs (can-tahs)

Desperation: Can tahs were statues of lower animals, such as coyotes, rats, spiders, and wolves, that had absorbed evil from Tak's ini.

The Dark Tower: The turtle sköldpadda was a can-tah, a little god.

can tah and can-tah take on other meanings:

[**Easter Egg**] *The Dark Tower*: Part of the phrase translated to "all breath comes from the woman" included "can-tah."

[**Easter Egg**] *The Dark Tower*: Powerful Manni incantations included "cah-tah."

[**Easter Egg**] *Black House*: Can-tah Abbalah = the Court of the Crimson King

[**Easter Egg**] *The Plant*: "Can tah" was among Carlos Detweiller's alien gibberish.

Charlie the Choo-Choo

The Dark Tower: In the Topeka, KS, of a world similar to ours, Gage Park had a Charlie the Choo-Choo ride. Charlie was also the main character of *Charlie the Choo-Choo* by Beryl Evans / Claudia Inez y Bachman.

Cell: The Northern Counties Expo had a Charlie the Choo-Choo among its rides.

John Law

"If It Bleeds": A courtroom TV show featuring Judge John Law.

Later: a courtroom TV show

Billy Summers: a courtroom show on daytime TV

Micmac Indians burial sites

Pet Sematary: This story revolves around a burial ground the Micmac Indians believed had soured.

The Tommyknockers: The Micmac Indians buried their dead in the woods near Ludlow, ME.

Nozz-A-La cola

The Dark Tower: 1) After leaving the Green Palace, the ka-tet found lunches in their packs, which included Nozz-A-La. 2) Jake found an empty Nozz-A-La bottle on the path to the Dogan, Outpost 16. 3) Mia's ATV had a six-pack minus a bottle. 4) In Fedic, Nigel the Butler served lunch with Nozz-A-La. 5) Ted Brautigan left food, including Nozz-A-La, for Roland, et al.

"Under the Weather": Brad Franklin's assistant Billy Ederle drank Nozzy from the machine.

The Ritual of Chüd

Two entities symbolically bite each other's tongues, then engage in a telepathic battle of wills. The first to let go may or may not be hurt, but will have no power over the other.

IT: As Bill Denbrough hurtled through the void toward the deadlights, he weakened IT with the Ritual enough to defeat its physical form.

Later: The Ritual helped Jamie Conklin keep the deadlight infesting Ken Therriault away. Until called upon.

Sharp Cereals

Cujo: The Sharp Company made Sharp Cereals. Admen Vic Trenton and Roger Breakstone took a damage-control tour after Red Razberry Zingers went out with a bad dye that made it look as if children vomited blood.

End of Watch: Sharp Cereals sponsored 'Round Here's last two tours.

Takuro Spirit

The Dark Tower: In the Topeka, KS, of a world similar to ours, Eddie Dean, et al, saw a Takuro Spirit automobile.

_11/22/63_: When Jake Epping returned from the Land of Ago, he saw a Ford Breeze, a Honda Zephyr, and a Takuro Spirit.

Putting it All Together—Part I

Now that we have a generous collection of connections, let's see how many works we can link into one amorphous blob.

Our base starts with works set in and mentioning Castle Rock:

The Stand
The Dead Zone
Cujo
"Rita Hayworth and Shawshank Redemption"
"The Body"
"Stud City"
"Mrs. Todd's Shortcut"
"Nona"
"Uncle Otto's Truck"
"Gramma"
IT
The Dark Half
"The Sun Dog"
Needful Things
Gerald's Game
"It Grows on You"
Bag of Bones
The Girl Who Loved Tom Gordon
Dreamcatcher
"The Man in the Black Suit"
"Riding the Bullet"
Lisey's Story
Blaze
"N."
Under the Dome
"A Good Marriage"
"Premium Harmony"

"Squad D"
Gwendy's Button Box
Elevation
Gwendy's Magic Feather
Gwendy's Final Task

IT is set in Derry, so we can bring in the others set in and mentioning Derry:

The Running Man
Pet Sematary
The Tommyknockers
"Secret Window, Secret Garden"
Dolores Claiborne
Insomnia
Hearts in Atlantis
"Autopsy Room Four"
"The Road Virus Heads North"
"Mute"
"Fair Extension"
11/22/63
"On Slide Inn Road"
"Rat"

Kids in "The Body" hiked to Harlow, a town we see again in:

"Drunken Fireworks"

"Secret Window, Secret Garden" takes place at Tashmore Lake in Tashmore, which allows us to add:

The Colorado Kid
Cell

Dreamcatcher references Jerusalem's Lot, so that brings in:

'Salem's Lot

"Jerusalem's Lot"
"One for the Road"
Doctor Sleep
Revival
The Institute

The Dark Father appears in *'Salem's Lot* and:

"Sometimes They Come Back"

Dolores Claiborne lived on Little Tall Island, so we get:

Storm of the Century

The Dead Zone had Cleaves Mills, and so does:

"The Lonesome Death of Jordy Verrill" / "Weeds"

The Stand's Arnette, TX, and Stovington, VT give us:

The Shining
"The Monkey"
Desperation
"Everything's Eventual"

With *The Shining* taking place so near Sidewinder, CO, so we add:

The Talisman
Misery
American Vampire

Jack Sawyer from *The Talisman* shows up in its sequel:

Black House

The Talisman's scene in Paradise Falls brings in:

Christine

Christine featured Horlicks University, as did:

"The Crate"
"The Raft"

11/22/63 had a Quik-Flash, and so did:

"Herman Wouk Is Still Alive"

Kirsten Carver wore a *MotoKops 2200* shirt, which links:

The Regulators

Rick Dees wanted Johnny Smith to be an *Inside View* psychic, which gives us these other stories mentioning the tabloid:

Needful Things
"The Night Flier"
"Popsy"
"Home Delivery"
From a Buick 8
The Dark Tower
"Big Driver"
Joyland
End of Watch
"If It Bleeds"
Billy Summers

Holly Gibney from *End of Watch* also appears in:

Mr. Mercedes
Finders Keepers
The Outsider

Mr. Mercedes had a Zoney's GoMart, as does:

Sleeping Beauties
"The Life of Chuck"

Dooling, WV, from *Sleeping Beauties* had a Shopwell; Maine had one in:

The Long Walk

Dreamcatcher introduces us to the Mile 81 rest area; we see it again in:

"Mile 81"

With a brief mention of Dennis and Thomas in *The Dark Tower*, we get:

The Eyes of the Dragon

Several works mention Stephen King as a real person. *The Dark Tower*, however, includes him as a character, as do:

"The Rock and Roll Dead Zone"
"Blockade Billy"

Four Fathers in *The Dark Tower* was also a restaurant/bar in:

"The Ballad of the Flexible Bullet"
The Plant

"Rita Hayworth and Shawshank Redemption" features Shawshank. It also gets a mention in:

"The Fifth Quarter"

Andy Dufresne is a major character in "Rita Hayworth and Shawshank Redemption". He is also mentioned in:

"Apt Pupil"

"Apt Pupil" mentions Springheel Jack, the antagonist in:

"Strawberry Spring"

The Shop covered up Haven's Tommyknocker problem, which links:

Firestarter
"The Langoliers"

The Tommyknockers mentions the Arrowhead installation, which we know from:

"The Mist"

"The Mist" has the Bridgton Pharmacy, as does:

"The King Family and the Wicked Witch"

In *'Salem's Lot*, Chamberlain and Gates Falls are nearby, which link:

Sword in the Darkness
Carrie
Rage
"Graveyard Shift"
Hearts in Atlantis
"Mr. Harrigan's Phone"

Carrie's mother worked at the Blue Ribbon Laundry, which brings in:

"The Mangler"
Roadwork

Low men in yellow coats showed up in *Hearts in Atlantis* and:

"Ur"

IT shows the GS&WM running through Derry, which gives us:

Cycle of the Werewolf

The Ritual of Chüd features in *IT* and:

Later

IT also mentioned a calming water in a Texas town, so we can link:

"The End of the Whole Mess"

IT's Bill Denbrough and Richie Tozier are mentioned in:

Duma Key

Mother Abagail lived in Hemingford Home, which allows us to link:

"The Last Rung on the Ladder"
"1922"
"Afterlife"
"Mister Yummy"

The Dark Tower featured Nozz-A-La soda, which gives us a link to:

"Under the Weather"

Gordie and Denny Lachance had body-surfed at Harrison State Park, which connects:

"Night Surf"

Richie Ginelli was in The Dark Tower and in:

Thinner

Dewey the Deck wouldn't get on the bad side of the Organization, so we add in:

"Battleground"
"The Ledge"

Henry Bowers spending time at Juniper Hill gives us:

"Suffer the Little Children"

The Stand uses God and Jim Morrison as characters (as opposed as merely mentioning the real-life figures), as do:

"An Evening at God's"
"The Beggar and the Diamond"
"You Know They Got a Hell of a Band"

We meet novelist Paul Sheldon in *Misery*. His readers appear in:

"The Library Policeman"
Rose Madder

"The Library Policeman" tells us about the library police. We see a police officer as a library policeman in:

"Morality"

<u>UNCONNECTED WORKS</u>

Novels that don't connect:

The Green Mile

Night Shift stories that don't connect:

"The Boogeyman"
"Gray Matter" (but there's an Easter Egg)
"I Am the Doorway"
"I Know What You Need"
"The Lawnmower Man"
"The Man Who Loved Flowers"
"Quitters, Inc."
"Trucks"
"The Woman in the Room"

Skeleton Crew stories that don't connect:

"Beachworld"
"Big Wheels: A Tale of the Laundry Game (Milkman #2)"
"Cain Rose Up"
"Do the Dead Sing?"/"The Reach"
"Here There Be Tygers"
"The Jaunt" (but there's an Easter Egg)
"The Man Who Would Not Shake Hands"
"Morning Deliveries (Milkman #1)"
"The Reaper's Image"
"Survivor Type"
"The Wedding Gig"
"Word Processor of the Gods"/"The Word Processor"

Creepshow stories that don't connect:

"Father's Day"
"Something to Tide You Over"
"They're Creeping Up on You"

Different Seasons novellas that don't connect:

"The Breathing Method"

Nightmares & Dreamscapes stories that don't connect:

"Chattery Teeth"
"Crouch End"
"Dedication"
"The Doctor's Case"
"Dolan's Cadillac"
"The House on Maple Street"
"The Moving Finger"
"My Pretty Pony"
"Rainy Season"
"Sneakers"

"Sorry, Right Number"
"The Ten O'Clock People"
"Umney's Last Case"

Everything's Eventual stories that don't connect:

"All That You Love Will Be Carried Away"
"The Death of Jack Hamilton"
"In the Deathroom"
"L.T.'s Theory of Pets"
"Lunch at the Gotham Café"
"That Feeling, You Can Only Say What It Is In French"
"1408"
"Luckey Quarter"

Just After Sunset stories that don't connect:

"Willa"
"The Gingerbread Girl"
"Harvey's Dream"
"Rest Stop"
"Stationary Bike"
"The Things They Left Behind"
"Graduation Afternoon"
"The Cat From Hell"
"*The New York Times* at Special Bargain Rates"
"Ayana"
"A Very Tight Place"

The Bazaar of Bad Dreams stories that don't connect:

"Batman and Robin Have an Altercation"
"The Dune"
"Bad Little Kid"
"A Death"
"The Bone Church"

"Tommy"
"The Little Green God of Agony"
"Cookie Jar"
"That Bus is Another World"
"Obits"
"Summer Thunder"

Putting it All Together—Part II

This chapter shows the connections in each novel.

CARRIE

Chamberlain, ME
Motton, ME
the Blue Ribbon Laundry

'SALEM'S LOT

Jerusalem's Lot, ME
Chamberlain, ME
Gates Falls, ME
Harlow, ME
Los Zapatos, Mexico
Kurt Barlow
Matt Burke
Father Donald Callahan
Dr. Cody
Miss Loretta Coogan
the Dark Father
Mr. Flip
Danny Glick
Ben Mears
Susan Norton
Mark Petrie
Richard Straker

THE SHINING

Sidewinder, CO
Stovington, VT

The Overlook
Stovington Preparatory Academy
Dick Hallorann
Danny Torrance
Jack Torrance

As the following connect to *Doctor Sleep*, *The Shining*'s sequel, you might not consider them connections:

Mrs. Brant
Horace Derwent
Lloyd
Mrs. Massey
Tony
Brett Torrance
Mark Torrance
Mike Torrance
Wendy Torrance
Harvey Watson

Rage

Gates Falls, ME
Harlow, ME

The Stand

Arnette, TX
Hemingford Home, NE
Castle Rock, ME
Haven, ME
Stovington, VT
Cheery Petroleum Company
the Organization
the Shop

Mother Abagail
Roberta Anderson
the dark man
God as a character
Randall Flagg
Jim Morrison as a character
The Trashcan Man

The Long Walk

Shopwell

The Dead Zone

Castle Rock, ME
Cleaves Mills, ME
Gates Falls, ME
Jerusalem's Lot, ME
Stovington, VT
Inside View
Quik-Pik
Stovington Preparatory Academy
Sheriff Bannerman
Katrina Bannerman
David Bright
Castle Rock Cougars
Rick Dees
Billy Dodd
Frank Dodd
Henrietta Dodd
Carol Dunbarger
Mary Kate Hendrasen
Roscoe Fisher
Alma Frechette
Cheryl Moody

Etta Ringgold
Rusty
Ann Simons
Johnny Smith
Greg Stillson
Pauline Toothaker

FIRESTARTER

the Organization
the Shop
Charlie McGee

ROADWORK

the Blue Ribbon Laundry
the Organization

CUJO

Castle Rock, ME
the Bridgton Pharmacy
Sheriff Bannerman
Katrina Bannerman
Joe Camber
Brett Camber
Charity Camber
Aunt Evvie Chalmers
the Castle Rock Cougars
Cujo
Frank Dodd
Henrietta Dodd
Carol Dunbarger
Roscoe Fisher
Alma Frechette

Mary Kate Hendrasen
Cheryl Moody
Gary Pervier
Etta Ringgold
Rusty
John Smith
Pauline Toothaker
Donna Trenton
Tad Trenton
Sharp Cereals

THE RUNNING MAN

Derry, ME
Harding

CHRISTINE

Paradise Falls, OH
Rocksburg, PA
Horlicks University
Christine
Mike Latimer

PET SEMATARY

Derry, ME
Haven, ME
Jerusalem's Lot, ME
Ludlow, ME
an Orinco truck
Gage Creed
Cujo
the Digger nickname for cemetery workers
the Micmac burial ground

THE TALISMAN

Arcadia Beach, NH
Oatley, NY
Paradise Falls, OH
Sidewinder, CO

As the following connect to *Black House*, *The Talisman*'s sequel, you might not consider them connections:

Lily Cavanaugh
Queen Laura DeLoessian
the Digger nickname for cemetery workers
Elroy
Captain Farren
Sunlight Gardener Scripture
Osmand
Speedy Parker
Parkus
Jack Sawyer
Lily Sawyer
Phil Sawyer
Morgan of Orris
Morgan Sloat
Richard Sloat
Smokey Updike
Wolf

THINNER

Richie Ginelli
Lemkes
Starbirds

Cycle of the Werewolf

Tarker's Mills, ME
the GS&WM railroad

IT

Derry, ME
Castle Rock, ME
Cleaves Mills, ME
Gatlin, NE
Haven, ME
Hemingford Home, NE
La Plata, TX
the GS&WM railroad
Juniper Hill
an Orinco chemical-fertilizer truck
Shawshank State Prison
Butch Bowers
The Bradley Gang
Christine
Dorsey Corcoran
Eddie Corcoran
Bill Denbrough
George Denbrough
Frank Dodd
Alma Frechette
Pauline Toothaker
Cheryl Moody
Carol Dunbarger
Etta Ringgold
Mary Kate Hendrasen
Adrian Mellon
Steven Dubay

John Garton
Dick Hallorann
Mike Hanlon
Ben Hanscom
Patrick Hockstetter
Eddie Kaspbrak
Norbert Keene
The Losers
Richard Macklin
Beverly Marsh
Officer Aloysius Nell
Rebecca Paulson
Pennywise
Richie Tozier
Phil Tracker
Tony Tracker
Chris Unwin
Stan Uris

THE EYES OF THE DRAGON

Delain
the Plains of Leng
Dennis
Flagg
Niner
King Roland
Thomas

MISERY

Sidewinder, CO
the Overlook Hotel
Designated Gawkers
Misery Chastain

Paul Sheldon
Jack Torrance
Annie Wilkes

THE TOMMYKNOCKERS

Arcadia Beach, NH
Arnette, TX
Cleaves Mills, ME
Derry, ME
Haven, ME
Ludlow, ME
the Arrowhead installation
Juniper Hill
the Shop
David Bright
Roberta Anderson
Designated Gawkers
Charlie McGee
'Becka Paulson
Pennywise
Johnny Smith
Stillson
the Micmac burial ground

THE DARK HALF

Castle Rock, ME
Derry, ME
Gates Falls, ME
Harlow, ME
Ludlow, ME
Juniper Hill
an Orinco truck
Sheriff Bannerman

Liz Beaumont
Thad Beaumont
Wendy Beaumont
William Beaumont
Deke Bradford
Sheila Brigham
Polly Chalmers
Deputy Andy Clutterbuck
Cujo
the Digger nickname for cemetery workers
Frank Dodd
Carol Dunbarger
Charlie Fortin
Alma Frechette
Homer Gamache
Mary Kate Hendrasen
Sonny Jackett
Bill Keeton
Danforth Keeton
Deputy John LaPointe
Cheryl Moody
Sheriff Pangborn
Annie Pangborn
Todd Pangborn
Lieutenant Henry Payton
Dave Phillips
Norris Ridgewick
Etta Ringgold
George Stark
Seat Thomas
Pauline Toothaker
Dr. Ray Van Allen

Needful Things

Castle Rock, ME
Derry, ME
Gates Falls, ME
Junction City, IA
the Plains of Leng
Inside View
Juniper Hill
Shawshank Prison
Sheriff George Bannerman
Thad Beaumont
Liz Beaumont
Wendy Beaumont
William Beaumont
Deke Bradford
Sheila Brigham
Brett Camber
Charity Camber
Joe Camber
Aunt Evvie Chalmers
Polly Chalmers
Chris Chambers
Deputy Andy Clutterbuck
Melissa Clutterbuck
Mr. Constantine
Cujo
Frank Dodd
Carol Dunbarger
Teddy Duchamp
Charlie Fortin
Alma Frechette
Homer Gamache
Mary Kate Hendrasen

Naomi Higgins
Sonny Jackett
Bill Keeton
Gordie Lachance
Deputy John LaPointe
Ace Merrill
Pop Merrill
Cheryl Moody
Sheriff Alan Pangborn
Annie Pangborn
Todd Pangborn
Lenny Partridge
Lieutenant Henry Payton
Sam Peebles
Gary Pervier
Dave Phillips
Norris Ridgewick
Etta Ringgold
Johnny Smith
George Stark
Vern Tessio
Seat Thomas
Pauline Toothaker
Donna Trenton
Tad Trenton
Dr. Ray Van Allen

GERALD'S GAME

Castle Rock, ME
Chamberlain, ME
Dark Score Lake in Maine
Derry, ME
Harlow, ME

Kashwakamak Lake
Motton, ME
Tashmore Glen, ME
Juniper Hill
Jessie Burlingame
Hollis
Raymond Andrew Joubert
Deputy John LaPointe
Jessie Mahout
Virginia Norey
Alan Pangborn
Norris Ridgewick
Dolores St. George

DOLORES CLAIBORNE

Dark Score Lake in Maine
Derry, ME
Jerusalem's Lot, ME
Little Tall Island, ME
Jessie Burlingame
Dolores Claiborne
Jessie Mahout
Virginia Norey
Dolores St. George
Joe St. George
Selena St. George
the *Island Princess* ferry

INSOMNIA

Derry, ME
Haven, ME
Ludlow, ME
Acadia Mental Health Hospital

the GS&WM
Inside View
Juniper Hill
Butch Bowers
Gage Creed
The Crimson King
Patrick Danville
Susan Day
Ed Deepneau
Mike Hanlon
Ben Hanscom
Ray Joubert
Adrian Mellon
Officer Aloysius Nell
Officer Chris Nell
Lois Roberts
Ralph Roberts
Roland
Joe Wyzer

Rose Madder

the City of Lud
Daughters and Sisters
Norman Daniels
Rose Daniels
Susan Day
Gert Kinshaw
Paul Sheldon
Cynthia Smith
Anna Stevenson

The Green Mile

None

Desperation

Arnette, TX
Wentworth, OH
Daughters and Sisters
Inside View's
MotoKops 2200
Norman Daniels
Rose Daniels
Gert Kinshaw
Paul Sheldon's book *Misery in Paradise*
Cynthia Smith
Anna Stevenson
can tahs

The Regulators

Wentworth, OH
MotoKops 2200

Bag of Bones

Castle Rock, ME
Dark Score Lake in Maine
Derry, ME
Gates Falls, ME
Harlow, ME
Kashwakamak, ME
Kewadin Pond in Maine
Motton, ME
TR-90 in Maine
TR-100 in Maine
TR-110 in Maine
Inside View
Juniper Hill

Shawshank Prison
Shopwell
Thad Beaumont
William Denbrough
Michael Noonan
Alan Pangborn
Norris Ridgewick
Lois Roberts
Ralph Roberts
Starbirds
George Stark
Joe Wyzer

STORM OF THE CENTURY

Little Tall Island, ME
Dolores Claiborne
Joe St. George
Danny Torrance

THE GIRL WHO LOVED TOM GORDON

Castle, ME
Motton, ME
TR-90 in Maine
TR-100 in Maine
TR-110 in Maine
Richie "Records" Tozier

HEARTS IN ATLANTIS

Derry, ME
Gates Falls, ME
Harwich, CT
Ted Brautigan

Breakers
The Crimson King
the Cumberlands
Bobby Garfield
Carol Gerber
the Library Police
low men
John Sullivan

DREAMCATCHER

Castle Rock, ME
Derry, ME
Jerusalem's Lot, ME
the Mile 81 rest area
the Bridgton Pharmacy
Shawshank Prison
Bill Denbrough
Steven Dubay
John Garton
Mike Hanlon
Ben Hanscom
Eddie Kaspbrak
The Losers' Club
Bev Marsh
Adrian Mellon
Officer Chris Nell
Pennywise
Richie Tozier
Phil Tracker
Tony Tracker
Chris Unwin
Stan Uris

Black House

the Dark Tower
French Landing, WI
Oatley, NY
Abbalah
Blaine
Ted Brautigan
Breakers
The Crimson King
The Little Sisters
Patricia
Roland
slow mutants
the Speaking Demon

As this is the sequel to *The Talisman*, you might not consider the following connections:

Lily Cavanaugh
Queen Laura DeLoessian
Elroy
Captain Farren
Sunlight Gardener Scripture
Osmand
Speedy Parker
Parkus
Jack Sawyer
Lily Sawyer
Phil Sawyer
Morgan of Orris
Morgan Sloat
Richard Sloat
Smokey Updike
Wolf

From a Buick 8

Rocksburg, PA
Horlicks University
Inside View

The Colorado Kid

Tashmore Lake in Tashmore, ME

Cell

Kashwakamak, ME
Kashwakamak Lake
Tashmore, ME
TR-90, ME
Juniper Hill
Charlie the Choo-Choo

Lisey's Story

Castle Rock, ME
Cleaves Mills, ME
Dark Score Lake in Maine
Derry, ME
Motton, ME
Shooter's Knob, TN
Tashmore Pond, ME
Acadia Mental Health Hospital
Michael Noonan
Deputy Andy Clutterbuck
Norris Ridgewick

Blaze

Castle Rock, ME
Harlow, ME
Federal Foods, Inc.
Portland General Hospital
Quik-Pik
Shawshank State Prison

Duma Key

R. Tozier
W. Denbrough

Under the Dome

Castle Rock, ME
Chester's Mill, ME
Derry, ME
Harlow, ME
Motton, ME
Tarker's Mills, ME
TR–90
the Chester's Mill *Democrat*
Shawshank State Prison
Julia Shumway

American Vampire

Sidewinder, CO

11/22/63

Arnette, TX
Castle Rock, ME

Derry, ME
Haven, ME
Quik-Flash store
Shawshank State Prison
Bowers
Dorsey Corcoran
Eddie Corcoran
George Denbrough
Ben Hanscom
Patrick Hockstetter
Norbert Keene
Lemkes
Dicky Macklin
Beverly Marsh
Starbirds
Richie Tozier
Phil Tracker
Tony Tracker
Takuro Spirit

THE DARK TOWER

the Dark Tower
Delain
French Landing, WI
Harwich, CT
Jerusalem's Lot, ME
the City of Lud
Los Zapatos, Mexico
Four Fathers
Inside View
the Sombra Corporation
the Tet Corporation
Mother Abagail

Kurt Barlow
Blaine
Ted Brautigan
Breakers
Matt Burke
Father Donald Callahan
Misery Chastain
Father Cody
Miss Loretta Coogan
the Crimson King
Cujo
Patrick Danville
the dark man
Ed Deepneau
Dennis
Dinky Earnshaw
Flagg
Randall Flagg
Mr. Flip
Bobby Garfield
Carol Gerber
Ginelli
Danny Glick
Stephen King
The Little Sisters
low men in yellow coats
Ben Mears
Niner
Susan Norton
Patricia
Mark Petrie
Ralph Roberts
Roland
King Roland

Mr. Sharpton
Paul Sheldon
slow mutants
The Speaking Demon
Greg Stillson
Sully-John
Richard Straker
taheen
Thomas
Jack Torrance
The Trashcan Man
Annie Wilkes
can-tahs
Charlie the Choo-Choo
Nozz-A-La
Takuro Spirit

JOYLAND

GS&WM
Inside View
Joyland
Hollywood Girls

DOCTOR SLEEP

Castle Rock, ME
Jerusalems' Lot, ME
Sidewinder, CO
Inside View
The Overlook Hotel
Stovington Preparatory Academy
Boyd
Dick Hallorann
Cam Knowles

Pete
'Round Here
Boyd
Steve
the True Knot

As this is the sequel to *The Shining*, you might not consider the following connections:

Mrs. Brant
Horace Derwent
Lloyd
Mrs. Massey
Tony
Brett Torrance
Jack Torrance
Mark Torrance
Mike Torrance
Wendy Torrance
Watson

Mr. Mercedes

Zoney's GoMart
Dr. Babineau
Boyd
Holly Gibney
Brady Hartsfield
Bill Hodges
Pete Huntley
Izzy Jaynes
Cam Knowles
Odell
Pete
Janey Patterson

Barbara Robinson
Jerome Robinson
Tanya Robinson
'Round Here
Henry Sirois
Steve
Elizabeth Wharton

REVIVAL

Castle Rock, ME
Gates Falls, ME
Harlow, ME
Jerusalem's Lot, ME
Motton, ME
Joyland
the Cumberlands
Hollywood Girls
Dorrance Marstellar

FINDERS KEEPERS

Finders Keepers
Zoney's GoMart
Dr. Babineau
Morris Bellamy
Dwight Cramm
Holly Gibney
Brady Hartsfield
Bill Hodges
Pete Huntley
Izzy Jaynes
Oliver Madden
Odell
Janey Patterson

Barbara Robinson
Jerome Robinson
Tanya Robinson
'Round Here

End of Watch

Finders Keepers
Inside View
Mrs. Babineau
Dr. Babineau
Holly Gibney
Brady Hartsfield
Bill Hodges
Pete Huntley
Izzy Jaynes
Cam Knowles
Odell
Barbara Robinson
Jerome Robinson
Tanya Robinson
'Round Here
Henry Sirois
Elizabeth Wharton
Sharp Cereals

Gwendy's Button Box

Castle Rock, ME
Cleaves Mills, ME
Dark Score Lake in Maine
Gates Falls, ME
Sheriff George Bannerman

Sleeping Beauties

Shopwell
Zoney's

The Outsider

Cheery Petroleum Company
Finders Keepers
Shopwell
Zoney's Go-Mart
Derek Anderson
Detective Ralph Anderson
Mrs. Babineau
Dr. Babineau
Morris Bellamy
Dwight Cramm
Holly Gibney
Brady Hartsfield
Bill Hodges
Jack Hoskins
Pete Huntley
Isabelle Jaynes
Oliver Madden
the outsider
Frankie Peterson
Jerome Robinson

Elevation

Castle Rock, ME
Inside View
Zoney's Go-Mart
Bannerman
the Night Flier

The Institute

TR-110 in Maine
Zoney's Go-Mart
walk-ins

Gwendy's Magic Feather

Castle Rock, ME
Derry, ME
Shawshank
Sheriff George Bannerman
Sheila Brigham
Frank Dodd
Sheriff Norris Ridgewick
Alan Pangborn

Later

John Law, a courtroom TV show
walk-in
the Ritual of Chüd

Billy Summers

Hemingford Home, NE
Sidewinder, CO
Inside View
the Overlook Hotel
Quik-Pik
Zoney's GoMart
John Law

GWENDY'S FINAL TASK

Castle Rock, ME
Dark Score Lake in Maine
the Tower
Derry, ME
Juniper Hill
the Sombra Corporation
the Tet Corporation
Sheila Brigham
The Bradley Gang
the Crimson King
low men
Pennywise
Norris Ridgewick
taheen

Easter Eggs

Self-Referential Easter Eggs

Richard Bachman

a Stephen King pseudonym

The Dark Tower: The character Stephen King wrote under the same pseudonym.

Donald M. Grant

Donald M. Grant published *The Dark Tower* books.

The Dark Tower: Calvin Tower mentioned Donald M. Grant editions of books.

Joe Hill

Stephen King's son and best-selling author

Sleeping Beauties: Dooling Correctional had Joe Hill paperbacks in the library.

Mr. Edwin King

Stephen King's middle name is Edwin, and he was a high-school English teacher. Stephen's father's middle name is Edwin, too.

Carrie: Mr. Edwin King taught English at Chamberlain Junior High School.

IT: Claude Heroux killed Eddie King with an ax.

Mr. Donald King

Stephen King's father is Donald King.

The Stand: Mr. Donald King, a traveling Electrolux salesman from Peru, IN, visited Mother Abagail.

Stephen King

"Slade": Steve King always made sure Jack Slade got there in time to save the day.

"The Night Flier": Stephen King readers enjoyed *Inside View*. [Note: The Stephen King reference was edited out of the version collected in *Nightmares & Dreamscapes*.]

Thinner: When Billy Halleck asked Dr. Houston about weird maladies affecting Duncan Hopley, Cary Rossington, and himself, the doctor thought Billy sounded like a Stephen King book.

Misery: Annie Wilkes bought Paul Sheldon an old typewriter from a time where there were "no celebrities doing ads for credit cards." Stephen King had done an AMEX commercial.

The Tommyknockers: A "fellow who lived up Bangor" wrote dirty words and about make-believe monsters.

The Dark Tower: 1) The Manhattan Restaurant of the Mind advertised Stephen King books on a chalkboard in the window. 2) Roland showed Donald Callahan *'Salem's Lot*, a novel with real-life details about Callahan. 3) Stephen King was a primary character.

John Swithen

Stephen King wrote "The Fifth Quarter" under the John Swithen pseudonym.

The cover and FULL DISCLOSURE introduction to *Blaze* tell us John Swithen was a Richard Bachman pseudonym.

Carrie: Maureen Cowen and John Swithen sang folk music at the Spring Ball.

Verrill

Chuck Verrill had been Stephen King's agent.

"Umney's Last Case": Verrill was Samuel D. Landry's literary agent.

Michael Whelan

Michael Whelan illustrated *The Dark Tower: The Gunslinger.*

"Stationary Bike": Richard Sifkitz named a man on his more-than-imaginary metabolism work crew Whelan, after Michael Whelan.

Blaze

The Talisman: Lily Cavanaugh received an Academy Award nomination for Best Supporting Actress for her performance in Blaze.

At the time of *The Talisman*'s publication, King's unpublished *Blaze* was well known. Later, Richard Bachman finished and published it.

Carrie (novel)

The Dead Zone: Patty Strachan, Chuck Chatsworth's girlfriend, accused Johnny Smith of telekinetically starting the Cathy's Roadhouse fire, "just like in that book *Carrie*."

The Dark Tower: 1) *Carrie* was Stephen King's first published novel. 2) Odetta Holmes started her period in gym class; other girls chanted, "Plug it UP!"

Carrie (movie)

The Dark Tower: Breaker Dinky Earnshaw said that people with special abilities were ostracized like Carrie at the prom.

Christine (movie)

Mr. Mercedes: Bill Hodges thought about the horror movie where an old Plymouth started on its own.

"Mile 81": Maine State Police Trooper Jimmy Golding saw *Christine* when he was a kid.

Cujo (novel)

The Dark Tower: The boy died in the book about Cujo.

Cujo (movie)

The Dark Tower: The boy lived in the movie about the Saint Bernard.

Creepshow

Insomnia: Ralph Roberts dreamed Carolyn was buried up to her neck on a beach ["Something to Tide You Over"] and black bugs poured from her mouth ["They're Creeping Up on You"].

The Dead Zone

Dreamcatcher: Lonesome Dave, reporting on WWVE-FM, cautioned people to avoid the grayboy-infested area north of Augusta, "the Hot Zone, the Dead Zone, or the Twilight Zone," whatever you want to call it.

***The Dead Zone* (novel)**

The Dark Tower: The character Stephen King wrote *The Dead Zone*.

***Desperation* (novel)**

The Dark Tower: The character Stephen King wrote *Desperation*.

"Donovan's Brain" (short story)

Dreamcatcher: Trapped in an office in his mind, Jonesy felt like Donovan's Brain in a tank of liquid. (Both could be referencing the 1942 movie, *Donovan's Brain*.)

***Golden Years* (miniseries)**

"Everything's Eventual": Dinky Earnshaw and his friend Pug watched *Golden Years* one summer.

Hearts in Atlantis **(collection)**

The Dark Tower: The character Stephen King wrote *Hearts in Atlantis*.

IT **(novel)**

The Dark Tower: The character Stephen King wrote *IT*.

IT **(movie)**

The Dark Tower: Bryan Smith thought the movie about the clown was very cool.

Mr. Mercedes: The Mercedes Killer's mask resembled Pennywise from the movie about the clown in the sewers.

Kingdom Hospital **(television series)**

Lisey's Story: When Lisey Landon told Deputy Alston she was on her way to see her sister in the hospital in Auburn, he asked whether it was CMG or Kingdom.

The Dark Tower: Character Stephen King considered *Kingdom Hospital* or *Rose Red* after *Storm of the Century*.

The Long Walk **(novel)**

The Dark Tower: The character Stephen King wrote *The Long Walk* under the Bachman pseudonym.

The Mist **(movie)**

Under the Dome: A blogger surmised the Dome was a government experiment gone wrong, like in the movie *The Mist*.

"The Old Dude's Ticker" (short story)

Dreamcatcher: Pete Moore remembered a story he had read in the eighth grade. A guy killed an old man because the old man's eye creeped him out.

On Writing

The Dark Tower: The character Stephen King wrote a how-to book on writing.

Pennywise from *IT* (movie, novel)

Elevation: A Castle Rock garage band called themselves Pennywise and the Clowns for the high school Halloween dance.

***Rose Red* (movie)**

Black House: A narrator flies us around French Landing showing us the sites. At one point, the narrator compares Black House with Shirley Jackson's Hill House and Rose Red in Seattle.

The Dark Tower: Character Stephen King considered *Kingdom Hospital* or *Rose Red* after *Storm of the Century*.

***'Salem's Lot* (novel)**

Blaze: John Cheltzman and Blaze went to see *Second Coming*, a vampire novel *Second Coming* was an early title for *'Salem's Lot*.

The Dark Tower: Roland showed Donald Callahan *'Salem's Lot*, a novel with real-life details about Callahan.

***The Shawshank Redemption* (movie)**

Finders Keepers: This was one of Holly Gibney's favorite movie soundtracks.

Later: Jamie Conklin thought Ken Therriault's apartment building looked somewhat like the prison in *Shawshank Redemption*.

***The Shining* (movie)**

The Dark Tower: Eddie Dean had seen *The Shining* and mentioned the creepy dead twins.

The Tommyknockers: Gard imagined himself bashing in the shed door with an ax like Jack Nicholson in *The Shining*.

The Outsider: Holly Gibney felt Mr. Kubrik's *Paths of Glory* was much better than *The Shining*.

The Institute: The Wilcox twins, standing off at a distance, reminded Luke Ellis of twin girls he had seen in an old horror movie.

***The Shining* (novel)**

The Regulators: Audrey Wyler's friend Kathi Goodlowe read two copies to tatters.

The Dark Tower: The character Stephen King wrote *The Shining*.

***The Stand* (novel)**

The Dark Tower: The character Stephen King wrote *The Stand*.

Storm of the Century (television series)

The Dark Tower: Character Stephen King considered *Kingdom Hospital* or *Rose Red* after *Storm of the Century*.

WKIT

Stephen and Tabitha King owned WKIT–FM 100.3 in Bangor, ME.

11/22/63: Ellen Dunning became a WKIT disc jockey.

WZON

Stephen and Tabitha King owned WZON–AM 620 in Bangor, ME.

The Tommyknockers: Gard picked up WZON through the steel plate in his head from a skiing accident.

IT: WZON played on Richie Tozier's Avis rental Mustang. On the morning of the big storm, WZON reported unusual weather conditions.

Places

Brickyard Hill

Carrie: Chamberlain, ME

The Long Walk: Porterville, ME

"The Body": Castle Rock, ME

Libertyville

The Dead Zone: Herb Smith worked on a new housing project in Libertyville, presumably in Maine.

Christine: This story takes place in Libertyville, PA.

Black House: French Landing, WI, had a Libertyville neighborhood.

Room 217

The Shining: Mrs. Massey died in the bathtub of the Overlook Hotel's Room 217.

Finders Keepers: Brady Hartsfield existed in Room 217 of the Lakes Region Traumatic Brain Injury Clinic.

Familiar Names

There are a handful of names that show up in more than one place, but their being the same character doesn't pan out for many. Some don't have enough information to establish a connection. Future works may close the gaps.

Mike Anderson

Storm of the Century: Constable Mike Anderson left Little Tall Island after the island gave his son away. He became a federal marshal in San Francisco.

"Obits": Journalist Mike Anderson wrote life-threatening obituaries for *Neon Circus*.

Patty Banning

"My Pretty Pony": This Patty was born around 1944, while . . .

Bag of Bones: . . . this Patty was born in 1960.

Norville Bates

Firestarter: a Shop agent

Needful Things: a short-order cook in San Francisco

Clay Blaisdell

Blaze: Law enforcement killed Clay after he kidnapped a baby.

The Dark Tower: Jake Chambers read a Clay Blaisdell Western.

John Brigham

Carrie: Margaret White's father, John, died in a shooting at his bar, The Jolly Roadhouse, in 1959.

Needful Things: Father John Brigham was the priest at Our Lady of Serene Waters in Castle Rock.

Henry Buck

Christine: An Albany used-car dealer, he took part in Will Darnell's smuggling operations.

The Tommyknockers: A Haven Tommyknocker, he worked at Paul's Down-East SuperMart in Bangor.

Clutterbuck

The Dark Half, "The Sun Dog," *Needful Things*, "It Grows on You," *Lisey's Story*: Andy Clutterbuck, a Castle Rock deputy

Blaze: Gerald Clutterbuck, a Castle Rock real estate agent

the Dark Witch of the Coos / Rhea of the Cöos

The Eyes of the Dragon: Rhiannon, also known as the Dark Witch of the Coos, was a character in an old wives' tale in Delain. When it was very windy, people said she was riding her broom.

The Dark Tower: Rhea of the Cöos, a very real witch in Hambry, Mejis, was young Roland's nemesis.

Martin Coslaw

Cycle of the Werewolf: Wheelchair-bound, he defeated the Beast.

Blaze: Hetton House Headmaster

Howard (Howie) Cottrell

The Shining: a Colorado snow-plow driver

"Autopsy Room Four": a Derry stockbroker

Arlene Cullum

The Tommyknockers: A Haven resident, she sold Amway products with the passion of a true believer.

Dolores Claiborne: Mrs. Arlene Cullum, of Little Island, babysat Selena St. George.

Bag of Bones: TR-90's Mrs. Arlene Cullum watched Kyra Devore while Mattie Devore worked.

Jimmy Cullum

IT: an IT victim

Blaze: moved south from Apex, ME

Billy deLois/DeLois

Carrie: On May 6, 1979, Billy deLois and Henry Trennant received two day's detention for cutting French I at Ewen Consolidated High School.

"The Raft:" Billy DeLois, a second-string football player, lived near Cascade Lake. Deke and Randy were Horlicks University students and had been roommates for three years. Deke played football and made the 1981 All-Conference football team. "The Raft" took place in October, so it could be 1982 or 1983. While it's possible the DeLoises moved from Chamberlain, ME, to Pennsylvania, there's just not enough information to say definitively.

Mrs. Sharon Denbrough

IT: Bill's mother, Sharon, had died before Bill returned to Derry in 1985.

"Fair Extension": Mrs. Denbrough lived next to Dave Streeter in 2001.

Roy DeWitt

"Mr. Harrigan's Phone": Roy grew up near Castle Rock and Harlow. He and Craig's father set off fireworks and ignited Frank Driscoll's kindling box.

"Rat": Roy's father ran the Big 90 General Store in Maine's unincorporated TR-90, then Roy did.

Peter Doyon

Needful Things: He and four other kids went to the Castle Rock vs. Greenspark Western Maine Schoolboy Championship game with Hugh Priest.

Dolores Claiborne: Little Tall Islander Peter Doyon put in a new well for the St. Georges when their old one went dry.

Teddy Duchamp

Carrie: Teddy Duchamp ran Teddy's Amoco on the corner of Main and Summer Streets in Chamberlain, ME. He died in 1968, and his son took over the station. These were Chamberlain Duchamps.

"The Body:" Teddy Duchamp died in a car crash in 1971 or 1972, so he's not the Teddy Duchamp that ran the Amoco. We don't know Teddy's son's name in *Carrie*, but could it have been Teddy, and if so, could he also be the Teddy in "The Body?" No, this Teddy's father was Norman Duchamp. These were Castle Rock Duchamps.

Tommy Erbter

Carrie: Carrie telekinetically knocked five-year-old Tommy off his bike in 1979.

Black House: Tommy Erbter is one of Tyler Marshall's friends. Ty was 10 in 2003, so Tommy would have been about the same.

Richard Farris

The Stand: Randall Flagg's men killed Judge Richard Farris on his was way to spy on Las Vegas for the Free Zone.

Gwendy's Button Box and the sequels: Richard Farris was the primary keeper of the button box. Not your average human being, his eyes changed color, and his palms had no lines.

Michael Fournier

Cujo: Castle Rock's postmaster in 1980.

"Home Delivery": Born around 1980, he was the first dead to rise from Jenny Island's graveyard.

Raymond Garraty

The Long Walk: Long Walker #47

Bag of Bones: a character in Mike Noonan's *My Childhood Friend* manuscript

Hanscom

Carrie: Vicky Hanscom, one of Carrie's classmates

IT: Ben Hanscom, a Loser

Blaze: Paul Hanscom, a Maine State Police Trooper

Bill/Billy Harris

Carrie: Billy Harris reported Chamberlain news.

Desperation: Bill Harris was Johnny Marinville's agent.

The Regulators: Bill Harris was Johnny Marinville's agent.

Note: Although characters in *Desperation* and *The Regulators* may share the same name and description, they were not the same characters.

George Hatfield

The Shining: A mediocre student at Stovington Preparatory Academy, he was expelled for slashing Jack Torrance's tires with a hunting knife.

The Talisman: He cheated at Thayer School, an offense for which they considered him for expulsion.

Patrick Hockstetter

Firestarter: a Shop doctor in 1982

IT: one of the troublemaker kids IT killed in 1958

Mrs. Kaspbrak

IT: Eddie's mother was a Mrs. Kaspbrak. Eddie had three aunts, one each in Bangor, Hampden, and Haven, ME. None of these aunts were named. Eddie's mother was close to them, so they probably were not Kaspbraks.

Misery: A Mrs. Kaspbrak lived across the street from Paul Sheldon in Lynn, MA. We don't know whether she's related to Eddie.

Billy Marchant/little Billy Marchant

Needful Things: Little Billy Marchant lived in Castle Rock in 1991.

Hearts in Atlantis: Billy Marchant played Hearts in Chamberlain Three's lounge in 1966.

Albert Martin

The Dark Half: Albert (Fuzzy) Martin's kids were grown, and his wife had left him. George Stark parked a Toronado in his barn.

Needful Things: Albert Martin, a lawyer and Cyndi Rose Martin's husband, could be Fuzzy's son. Or not.

Alice Maxwell

Cell: Alice Maxwell was born in 1988 and raised in Massachusetts. Her father ran a framing and print shop. She was killed in 2003.

Billy Summers: Alice Reagan Maxwell was born in 1998 and raised in Rhode Island. Her father owned a furniture store.

Peter McVries

The Long Walk: Walker #61

The Dark Tower: Peter McVries of Debaria was poisoned three years before the skin-man terrorized the town.

Sergeant Meggs

The Dead Zone: worked for the Maine State Police, Orono branch

"They're Creeping Up on You": a police officer

Mrs. Moran

IT: taught the fourth grade at Derry Elementary School

Bag of Bones: Mike Noonan's first-grade teacher in Prout's Neck, ME

Cathy Morse

Revival: Dan Jacobs selected Cathy Morse as a volunteer for a Lightning Portrait at the Tulsa State Fair.

"Bad Little Kid": Cathy Morse was a classmate of Marlee Jacobs at the Mary Day Grammar School in Talbot, AL.

Stan Norris

"The Ledge": Cressner found out about this bachelor tennis pro's affair with his wife, Marcia.

The Stand: Stan and his family caught Captain Trips from Henry Trent outside Babe's Kwik-Eat.

Father O'Brian

Rose Madder: Father O'Brian was a priest in Aubreyville.

IT: Father Ashley O'Brian was a Shawshank State Prison Catholic priest.

Richard (Dicky) Osgood

Bag of Bones: Richard was a Motton real estate agent in the 1990s.

Revival: In the 1960s, Dicky went to Harlow's one-room school on Route 9. (Did he become a real estate agent when he grew up?)

Freddy Overlock

Carrie: Freddy Overlock was one of the high school guys among Henry Black, Billy Nolan, and others in 1979.

'Salem's Lot: Freddy Overlock's daughter, Judy, ran off with a Saladmaster salesman in 1957 or 1958. Freddy would have to have been in at least his thirties. In 1979, he would have been well over fifty.

Philly Loubird

IT: Mike Hanlon's uncle, Philly Loubird Hanlon, grew up in North Carolina and became a Tucson, AZ, City Council member.

"Mr. Harrigan's Phone": Old Philly Loubird lived near Harlow, ME.

Charles Pritchett

'Salem's Lot: Charles V. and Amanda Pritchett bought the Griffen farm then moved away a month later because of funny noises.

Blaze: Charles Victor Pritchett, a drifter, was briefly a suspect in the Joseph Gerard IV kidnapping.

Jack Sawyer and Jack

The Talisman: In September 1981, Jack Sawyer, almost 13, and his mother moved to the Alhambra Inn and Gardens in Arcadia Beach, NH. In *Black House*, we learn that his mother, Lily, died of cancer.

The Tommyknockers: After a week-long drunken blackout in July 1988, Gard woke up on Arcadia Beach and talked with a kid who called himself Jack, who said his mother died in a car crash. While the boy reminds us of Jack Sawyer, Jack Sawyer would be 20 and no longer a kid on the beach. Also, we learn in *Black House* that the Sawyers had returned to Los Angeles and, by the time Jack was 16, he had blocked out his Travelin' Jack days, including those in New Hampshire.

Cora Simard

Carrie: a Chamberlain, ME, resident

"Gramma": Henrietta Dodd's friend

The Tommyknockers: a Haven, ME, resident

Al Stamper

Revival: This ex-soul singer had two ex-wives and assisted Charlie Jacobs at The Latches in upstate New York.

"Rat": Al retired as head of a college English Department for health reasons. His wife of forty-five years was with him until their end.

Laurel Stevenson

"The Langoliers": In August of 1990 or 1991, this Laurel was a teacher with a master's degree in library science.

Gerald's Game: In February 1993, this Laurel was a counselor/therapist. Jessie remembered her from her counseling with Nora Callighan in 1986.

Mrs. Sullivan

Hearts in Atlantis: Harwich, CT, resident with three sons, including Georgie and Sully-John

"Home Delivery": Little Tall Island, ME, resident, with husband, George, and daughter, Maddie

Insomnia: Derry, ME, resident, with son, Pete

Stuttering Bill

IT: As a child, Bill Denbrough stuttered.

The Dark Tower: After the world moved on, Bill the Maintenance Robot was nicknamed Stuttering Bill.

Jackie Talbot

Carrie: a male born in the early 1960s

'Salem's Lot: a female born in the early 1950s

Mrs. Thomas

IT: at Derry Elementary School

IT: at Chevrus High School in Portland

The Girl Who Loved Tom Gordon: a Sanford, ME, resident

The Turtle

IT: The Final Other created the Turtle, which supported the Losers but didn't interfere. The Turtle vomited and created the universe, then later choked on a galaxy and died.

The Dark Tower: One of the Twelve Guardians of the Beams, an important one, which the Great Old Ones created. The Turtle advised Roland.

11/22/63: 1) Beverly Marsh asked George Amberson whether he knew of the Turtle. 2) In 11/22/63 and in real life, General Edwin Walker lived at 4011 Turtle Creek Boulevard.

Phrases and Sayings

"DS" ("down south")

Joyland: In the Talk, DS, for "down south," meant leaving for good.

Revival: DS (down south) was carny-speak for getting out of town.

"DRT—Dead Right There"

The Dark Tower: Ambulance driver Julio Estavez referred to people who were DOA (Dead On Arrival) as DRT.

Duma Key: Xander Kamen had a heart attack at Starbucks. His brother said he was DRT.

"eventual"

"Everything's Eventual": Dinky Earnshaw's friend Pug used the word "eventual" instead of "awesome." Dinky included it in his own vocabulary. When he remarked that Mr. Sharpton's Mercedes was eventual, Mr. Sharpton replied, "everything's eventual, Dink."

The Dark Tower: Breaker Dinky Earnshaw thought Ted Brautigan was eventual.

"Rat": Drew Larson knew he'd resolve a minor plot problem in his new novel eventually because everything was eventual.

"five-by" and "five-by-five"

This is an actual term that originated with military radio communication to describe radio signal strength (the first five) and clarity (the second five). "Five by five" for "loud and clear" fell out of military use and became slang for "everything's OK." In the world of Stephen King, it is police code for "everything's OK."

From a Buick 8: Troop D used it.

Lisey's Story: The Castle Rock Sheriff's Office used this term, which Lisey was familiar with.

Under the Dome: Colonel Cox used it in the military communications sense.

Gwendy's Final Task: At T-minus-27, Gwendy replied "five-by-five" that all was good with her prior to liftoff.

"fushing feef!"

The Talisman: A spider in the Black Hotel screamed at Jack Sawyer.

"The Sun Dog": Kevin Delevan had a nightmare where a wino in Oatley, NY, shouted, "fushing feef!"

Black House: The hypothetical old homeless person with an empty shopping cart yells out.

"Getting Off A Good One"

IT: Richie Tozier called telling a good one-liner zinger (or ripping a loud fart) was "Getting Off A Good One."

The Colorado Kid: Stephanie McCann had "gotten off a good one" with a quick joke.

The Dark Tower: Straw Willem always snapped his suspenders when he thought he had "gotten off a good one," the swamp-dwellers chuckled as if Tim Ross had "gotten off an especially good one," and Will Wegg slapped his thigh as if Roland hand "gotten off a good one."

"A Good Marriage": Bob "chuckled as if she'd [Darcy] gotten off an exceptionally witty line."

"Give me what I want and I'll go away."

Storm of the Century: Andre Linoge wanted a protégé from Little Tall Island.

Hearts in Atlantis: Bobby Garfield wanted Len Files to give him Ted Brautigan's winnings.

"If It Bleeds": Chet Ondowsky wanted Holly Gibney's flash drive showing many of his outsider incarnations.

"God grant she/he lie still."

'Salem's Lot: The line appeared on Hubert Barclay Marsten's tombstone.

The Shining: Wendy Torrance thought it while watching Danny get some much-needed sleep.

"It Grows on You": Sarah Tamson Tabitha Francine Newall was born without arms but with fingers growing from her eye sockets; she died six hours later. Her epitaph read, "GOD GRANT SHE LIE STILL."

Bag of Bones: Mike Noonan remarked that "God grant she lye stille" appeared on old tombstones. He thought of it again after dealing with Sarah Tidwell.

The Dark Tower: Referring to Black Thirteen, Roland remarked, "Gods grant it sleep."

"He thrusts his fists against the posts and still insists he sees the ghosts."

IT: To ease his stuttering, Bill Denbrough recited this line.

'Salem's Lot: Mark Petrie recited it when Danny Glick hovered outside his bedroom window.

"I don't shut up I grow up. And when I look at you I throw up."

"The Body": one of many of the boys' friendly taunts

The Dark Tower: A young Eddie Dean and his pals often said this.

"Just call me Billie, everyone does"

"The Crate": Wilma (Billie) Northrup

The Dark Half: Wilhemina (Billie) Burks

Honorable Mention—*Firestarter*: Cap Hollister said, "Just call me Cap, everybody does."

Honorable Mention—*11/22/63*: Charles Frati told George Amberson, "But you can call me Chaz. Everyone does."

"long days and pleasant nights"

The Dark Tower: This was often said as a greeting or farewell. The response was "and may you have twice the number."

"A Fair Extension": While talking with Carl Goodhugh, Dave Streeter equated "life is good" with this.

"mess in with"

Insomnia: Dorrance Marstellar warned Ralph Roberts to not "mess in with" long-time business.

Doctor Sleep: An enraged Rose the Hat felt Abra Stone messed in with the wrong person.

"my pretty pony"

"My Pretty Pony": George Banning taught that saying, "my pretty pony," after each number while counting time takes about a second.

Dolores Claiborne: To not get tripped up while giving her statement, Dolores paused three seconds after each question, thinking, "my-pretty-pony," after each count.

"other worlds than these"

The Dark Tower: When Roland chose the Tower over Jack Chambers, the boy told him, "Go then. There are other worlds than these."

Insomnia: When someone's aura changed here, Clotho and Lachesis sent them on to other worlds than these.

"Low Men in Yellow Coats": After his adventure with Ted Brautigan, Bobby Garfield knew there were other worlds than this on the Tower.

Doctor Sleep: Dan Torrance told Dr. John Dalton that the shining was more than mere telepathy, as there were other worlds than these.

Under the Dome: Barbie when discussing the leatherheads: "The one thing I'm sure of is that there are other worlds than the ones we can see with our puny telescopes here on Earth."

Gwendy's Final Task: Three years after Gwendy disappeared in space, Mr. Peterson, gazing at the stars, heard the words, "there are other worlds than these."

"shut your pie-hole"

Did Stephen King coin this phrase, or does it have older origins?

Christine: Will Darnell to Arnie Cunningham

"The Raft": Deke to LaVerne

The Dark Half: George Stark to Liz Beaumont

Revival: Mr. Morton to Andy Morton

NINETEEN

Sometimes, a cigar is just a cigar, and sometimes, the number nineteen is just a number. Although we like to use nineteen to connect to *The Dark Tower*, we must remember nineteen is specific to Roland and his *ka-tet*. So, to connect another work using nineteen, we need to establish its significance to them. That leaves most 19s as just a number. As they remind us of *The Dark Tower*, they could be Easter eggs.

The Dark Tower:

—A Patrick Danville painting showed 19 steps rising from the base of the Dark Tower.

—When the group noticed 19 everywhere, they called themselves the Kat-Tet of Nineteen.

—Ka of Nineteen ruled the Keystone World.

—Federal Outpost 19 was near the Tower.

—19 of around two hundred derricks still pumped in the Citgo oil patch outside Hambry, Mejis.

—19 counts from turning back and leaving the Endless Forest, Tim Ross saw the Covenant Man's campfire.

—Directive Nineteen prohibited DARIA from giving certain information to Tim Ross without a password.

—Jake Chambers selected two books from a table in The Manhattan Restaurant of the Mind, leaving 19.

—The last group of Wolves was trapped on the arroyo path. It numbered 19.

—KidzPlay owed their accountants $69,211.19 (dollars digits sum to 19; cents is 19)

—The Tet Corporation gave Roland a gold Patek Philippe watch costing 19 thousand dollars.

—The diesel pump counter behind the East Stoneham General Store reset to 0019.

—Susannah Dean put a bag of 19 Oriza plates in their Plaza-Park Hotel safe. Jake Chambers used them in the Dixie Pig.

—"chassit" is 19

—595 doors to other worlds remained operational in Fedic.

—code to the Arc 16 Experimental Station Control Room: 25413121

—19 civil rights activists, including Odetta Holmes, stayed in Oxford, MS, after the disappearance of Cheney, Goodman, and Schwerner.

—Ted Brautigan guessed the number a doctor picked: 748

—In jail, Don Callahan saw graffiti about someone having their 19th nervous breakdown.

—"Nineteenth Nervous Breakdown" by the Rolling Stones blasted out of the Tower of Power record store.

—Before hitting Stephen King, Bryan Smith listened to Steely Dan sing "Hey Nineteen" and Owt-Ray-Juss perform "Gangsta Dream 19."

—It was 19 days' walk from Dandelo's hut to the Dark Tower.

—Lot #298 (digits sum to 19) Block #19 identified the vacant lot at the corner of Second Avenue and Forty-Sixth Street. The rose in the lot had 19 petals.

—The Sombra Corporation's Detroit office was at 982 Michigan Avenue.

—Susannah-Mia had room 1919 at the New York Plaza-Park Hotel.

—Calvin Tower and Aaron Deepneau stayed in Cabin #19 on Rocket Road in East Stoneham, ME.

—East Stoneham Meeting Hall, Built 1819 (digits sum to 19)

—19 Turtleback Lane was a site where many walk-ins came through.

—Don Callahan and Jake Chambers stowed Black Thirteen in Locker 883 beneath the World Trade Center.

—*Charlie the Choo-Choo* copyright: 1936

—Rowan Magruder then Donald Callahan in hospital room 577; Callahan was hospitalized on May 19.

—Donald Callahan died on December 19.

—Stefan Toren's dead-letter (will) was dated March 19, 1846.

—Breakers helped Sheemie check the date in the Keystone World. The time was 9:19 PM.

—Chip McAvoy's truck clock stopped at 9:19.

—Claudia y Inez Bachman
Ted Stevens Brautigan
Donald Frank Callahan
Wayne Dale Overholser
Richard Patrick Sayre
Benjamin Slightman Jr.

Carrie: Sue Snell lived at 19 Back Chamberlain Road.

The Shining:

—During Dick Hallorann's time at the Overlook Hotel, 19 guests stayed in the Presidential Suite.

—19 steps lead you from the lobby to the first level, and another 19 to the second.

—Mark Anthony Torrance
Robert Townley Watson

"Children of the Corn": 19 was the Age of Favor.

The Stand: Larry Underwood's group had 19 people when they arrived in the Free Zone.

The Long Walk: Raymond Davis Garraty

The Dead Zone: Sarah and Johnny placed bets on Sol Drummore's Wheel of Fortune. Both of Sarah's bets lost, but Johnny's six won. Johnny bet on a range of numbers until his last bet, where he put all on 19 and won.

Roadwork:

—Charles Dawes was diagnosed with a brain tumor 19 days after being admitted into Doctor's Hospital.

—The Daweses had to move to make way for an extension of Route 784.

"Rita Hayworth and Shawshank Redemption": Andy Dufresne was inmate 81433–SHNK.

Pet Sematary:

—Huey Garber's train delivered the coffins of 19 military personnel, including Timmy Baterman, in New England.

—David Roger Dandridge

Thinner: Lonesome Tommy McGhee

Needful Things: Ace Merrill and Dan Keeton's bombs killed 19 people in Castle Rock.

"Chattery Teeth": Bill Hogan was one of 19 passengers aboard a Wester Pride commuter flight that crashed near Reno, NV. Six passengers died; Bill suffered a broken back.

"Home Delivery": George Sullivan croaked while bowling lane 19.

The Green Mile: Brutal Howell logged Steamboat Willy's visit. Regulation 19 required logging each visitor to E Block.

Bag of Bones: Joanna left Mike Noonan the message, "go down nineteen." The first letter from each word on page 19 of his manuscript gave him, "owls undEr studIO."

Hearts in Atlantis: 19 of Chamberlain Three's thirty-two young men flunked out or moved to a different dorm because the semester-long Hearts epidemic.

Dreamcatcher: Derry Tiger quarterback Richie Grenadeau was #19.

"The Man in the Black Suit": Some time after catching and cleaning a 19-inch brook trout, nine-year-old Gary met the man in the black suit.

"Riding the Bullet": Jean Parker was in Central Maine Medical Center, room 487.

Cell:

—A small plane, tail number LN6409, crashed shortly after the Pulse hit.

—Gaiten Academy was established in 1846.

—Clay Riddell and his group picked up Route 19 in New Hampshire and followed it into Maine.

Blaze: The Gerard's estate had 19 steps between the first two stories.

Duma Key:

—Ilse Freemantle's Delta flight out of Sarasota: 559

—Edgar Freemantle's email handle: EFree19

—Pam Freemantle's email handle: Pamorama667

—Sandy Smith's email handle: SmithRealty9505

—Melinda Freemantle's Delta flight for Edgar's art show: 496

—last four digits of Wireman's phone number: 8191

—Bad Nineteen Music owned the rights to the lyrics of "Dig," performed by Shark Puppy.

"Mute": Barb Monette was an executive secretary with the Maine School Administrative District 19.

"N.":

—N. believed 19 to be a powerful and bad odd number.

—Don LeClair, Dr. John Bonsaint's brother-in-law, lived at 964 Lisbon Street.

—Charlie Keen's (a friend of John Bonsaint) email handle: keen1981

Under the Dome: Big Jim Rennie got Room 19 at Catherine Russell Hospital. Pamela Chen and Officer Morrison used Bus 19 to save people from the fire.

"1922": Wilfred James got a $35 loan to help his son. By Christmas, with interest, the payments would total thirty-eight dollars, $19 dollars for each.

"A Good Marriage":

—Donnie Anderson played in the District 19 Little League tournament.

—Darcy Madsen Anderson
Robert Emory Anderson

11/22/63:

—Al Templeton lived at 19 Vining Street.

—Jake Epping lived at 19 Bluebird Lane.

—The Dunnings lived at 379 Kossuth Street.

—Oswald's Hands Off Cuba flyers urged people to write to PO Box 1919 for information on meetings.

—a Plymouth Fury with Maine license plate: 90–811

—Jake's license plate: 23383 IY

—George Amberson's Social Security Number: 005–52–0223

—George Amberson rented safe deposit box 775.

—Jake Epping spent 19 cents at the Kennebec Fruit Company his first time back in the past.

—On his third trip, George Amberson spent seventeen dollars and 19 cents on various items from two stores near Tamarack Motor Court.

—George Amberson bought a 1954 Ford Sunliner.

—Althea Pierce Dunning

—A cribbage hand totaling 19 points is the impossible "mystic nineteen."

—George took US19 from Florida's Gulf Coast toward Mississippi.

—phone number on a sign to rent 4905 Magazine Street in New Orleans: MU3–4192

—George Amberson's Dallas phone number: WEstbrook 7–5430

—George de Mohrenschildt's office phone number: CHapel 5–6323

—May 19 was opening night for *Of Mice and Men*, and it was Marina and Lee Harvey Oswald's nineteenth day of marriage.

—Candlewood Bungalows

"The Turbulence Expert":

—Flight 19 from Boston, MA, to Sarasota, FL

—Flight 694 from Boston to Dallas, TX

Mr. Mercedes:

—Under Debbie's Blue Umbrella account names: kermitfrog19, otrelaw19

—Elizabeth Wharton lived in a 19th-floor condominium.

—The city's firearms code, section 19, specified a permit to carry must be carried along with the concealed weapon.

—Police Department main phone exchange: 1900

—Jerome Peter Robinson

Revival:

—Terry Morton and his father got an old 1951 Ford Running. They called it the Road Rocket, number 19.

—Charles Daniel Jacobs

Finders Keepers:

—Kermit William Hodges

—lock code to Drew Halliday's bookshop office: 9118

—Under Debbie's Blue Umbrella username and password for Bill Hodges: kermitfrog19

—Ruth Scapelli lived at 298 Tannenbaum Street.

"Mile 81":

—The Lussier family used to live at 19 Fresh Winds Way.

"Ur":

—Wesley Smith's birthday: July 19

"Herman Wouk Is Still Alive":

—A newspaper piece about Herman Wouk continued on page 19.

"Blockade Billy":

—Billy Blakely was Titans player number 19.

"Summer Thunder":

—Route 19 at Lake Pocomtuck in Vermont

Gwendy's Button Box:

—Gwendy's button box dispensed 1891 Morgan silver dollars.

Sleeping Beauties:

—Janice Tabitha Coates
Alexander Peter Bayer
Regina Alberta Wainer
Ursula Whitman-Davies

—Alfred Freeman lived at 19 Eldridge Street

—Kayleigh Rawlings was inmate #4521131–2

The Outsider:

—Terence John Maitland

—In 1845 (digits sum to 19), 19 students in a girls' school in Latvia watched as their teacher's doppelganger strode into the classroom and mimicked the teacher as the instructor wrote on the chalkboard.

Elevation:

—Deirdre McComb ran various races under the number 19.

Gwendy's Magic Feather:

—Gwendy found an 1891 Morgan silver dollar on her desk.

—Gwendy and her husband lived in Unit 19B of the Castle View Condominiums.

—Deborah Parker lived in the 1900 block of View Drive.

Later:

—Thumper had set 19 bombs without any deaths.

—code to Donnie Marsden's hidden door: 73612

—Liz Dutton's cell phone screenlock PIN: 2665

"Mr. Harrigan's Phone":

—The Dow Jones index hit 14,716 when Craig gave an iPhone to Mr. Harrigan.

"The Life of Chuck":

—Route 19 ran through Marty Anderson's town.

—Felicia Anderson lived at 19 Fern Lane.

"If It Bleeds":

—Mr. Dan Bell lived at 19 Lafayette Street in Portland, ME.

—security code to the side door of the building that housed Finders Keepers: 4753

"Rat":

—Drew Larson's email handle: drew1981@gmail.com

Billy Summers:

—Billy grew up at 19 Skyline Drive in Mayville, TN.

—Under the Dalton Smith alias, Billy lived at 658 Pearson Street.

—a Bucky Hanson communication alias: bigpapi982

—Hanson199, a youtube user name indicating Bucky Hanson at 199 Edgewood Mountain Drive

—the twisty Route 19 in the Colorado mountains (Note: Colorado does have a Route 19.)

—Nick Majarian lived at 1900 Cherokee Drive.

—Nick's safe-room code: 6247

—woodeyd667@gmail.com

—Roger Klerke lived at 775 Montauk Highway

—judyb14455@aol.com

—Shanice Anya Ackerman
Elmer Randolph Hanson
Catherine Ann Summers

Gwendy's Final Task:

—a Tet Corporation rocket: Eagle–19 Heavy

—Gwendy's space mission docked to the MF–1 space station for 19 days.

—lockbox combination: 1512253

—The button box dispensed 1891 Morgan silver dollars.

—Two chocolates from the box helped Gwendy ace a mental acuity test in 19 minutes.

MISCELLANEOUS EASTER EGGS

Army Accidents

"The Body": Denny Lachance was killed in Army Basic Training at Fort Benning, GA. An Army truck hit his Jeep.

The Green Mile: After Pearl Harbor, assistant warden Curtis Anderson he enlisted in the Army. He was killed in a truck accident at Fort Bragg.

Arnie's Girlfriend

Christine: While Leigh Cabot appeared to be Arnie Cunningham's love interest, Christine was his true girlfriend.

"Sorry, Right Number": An Arnie was the boyfriend of Christine, a Bolton prep school student.

becoming

The Tommyknockers: Tommyknocker becoming turned Haven, ME, residents into Tommyknockers.

The Dark Tower: Immortal being Mia underwent a becoming process to become mortal so she could carry and give birth to a child.

Doctor Sleep: The True Knot had a painful process called the Turning, where rubes become True Knot.

Berol Black Beauty Pencils

The Dark Half: George Stark wrote with Black Beauties.

Dreamcatcher: While everyone else used Eberhard Faber pencils, Beaver preferred Black Beauties.

Honorable Mention—*Misery*: The typewriter had thrown so many keys that Paul Sheldon finished Misery's Return longhand with Berol Black Warriors.

Honorable Mention—"Sneakers": Paul Jannings stabbed drug-dealer Sneakers in the right eye with a Berol Black Warrior pencil.

brain damage from special abilities

The Dead Zone: Johnny Smith

Firestarter: Andy McGee

The Dark Tower: Sheemie

Brownie's Stores

"It Grows On You": Bill "Brownie" McKissick, then his son, Harley" ran the store in Castle Rock, ME.

Under the Dome: Velma Winter ran the store in Chester's Mill, ME, after Dil Brown died.

11/22/63: Durham, ME

Revival: Duane Robichaud and his parents ran the store in Harlow, ME.

can-toi, can toi, and can-toi-tet

The Dark Tower: can-toi were human-like creatures with rat's heads. Ted Brautigan called them low men.

Desperation: The Tak-possessed Collie Entragian called wild animals *can-toi*.

The Dark Tower: Wild animals were called can-toi-tete.

Captain Trips

"Night Surf": Most people died from A6, a fatal Southeast Asia Flu most people caught. A6 was also called Captain Trips.

The Stand: Strain 848-AB, the highly communicable and deadly flu virus that escaped Project Blue's labs, also picked up the Captain Trips nickname.

The Dark Tower: A superflu ravaged the America of another world. It was called Captain Trips in California, and Tube-Neck in the Midwest.

Cars That Heal Themselves

Christine: As long as she was moving, Christine could repair almost any amount of damage.

From a Buick 8: The Buick repaired chips and scratches. No motion required.

College Card Addictions

The Regulators: Steve Ames flunked out of Boston University because of too much bridge-playing, booze, and Panama Red.

Hearts in Atlantis: A Hearts epidemic struck Chamberlain Three.

deadlights

IT: IT's true form was almost inconceivable to humans.

Insomnia: The Crimson King tried to stop Ralph Roberts from saving Patrick Danville and thousands of others. The Crimson King was blown into the deadlights when Ralph defeated him.

Later: A form of demon infested human spirits. To look into such a light meant instant insanity.

Death By Train-Car Smushing

The Dead Zone: Frank Dodd's father, drunk, died in a coupling accident between two flatcars.

Pet Sematary: René Michaud, a Bangor & Aroostook Railroad worker, was killed between two boxcars in a storm.

dim

Invisibility was impossible, but certain folks could make themselves dim to avoid being seen.

The Talisman: Wolfs and Osmond's son (Reuel Gardener's Twinner) could make themselves dim.

The Eyes of the Dragon: With a spell and a potion, Flagg could make himself dim. Only people who knew the dim one well could see them.

Insomnia: While gliding along the railroad tracks next to the golf course, Ralph thought he and Lois were dim when he saw the golfers didn't seem to notice them.

"Heavenly Shades of Night Are Falling": A friend of Carol Gerber's taught her the trick of being dim to make her good at not being seen.

Doctor Sleep: Silent Sarey had the knack of dimness. Only if you knew where she was and concentrated could you see her.

Emporium Galorium

"The Sun Dog": Pop Merrill was the proprietor of the Emporium Galorium, a junk-shop in Castle Rock.

Under the Dome: Julia Shumway called Ray Towle's Mill Used & New Books an emporium galorium.

Fading Memories

IT: After defeating IT, the Losers' memories of their experiences faded.

Insomnia: Lois Chasse and Ralph Roberts lost their memories of dealing with Ed Deepneau.

The Dark Tower: Susannah Dean's Mid-World memories began fading after going to the New York in a world similar to the one she was from.

Fratis and Pawnshops

IT: Frati Brothers pawnshop on Kansas Street

11/22/63: Marjorie and Charles Frati ran Mermaid Pawn & Loan on East Side Drive. Frank Frati and his daughter, Wanda, ran a pawnshop in Fort Worth, TX. All four were related.

"Heavenly shades of night are falling"

lyrics from a Platters song

The Dark Tower: Odetta Holmes sang this line.

Hearts in Atlantis: A story is titled "Heavenly Shades of Night Are Falling."

Hernando's Hideaway

"The Fifth Quarter": An outhouse behind Sarge's shack was labeled "Hernando's Hideaway."

Desperation: WELCOME TO HERNANDO'S HIDEAWAY was painted above a Desperation Mining Corporation garage door.

The Colorado Kid: The Cogan's had a HERNANDO'S HIDEAWAY plaque over their front door in Nederland, CO.

Infinitely Large Structures Inside

"The Breathing Method": From the outside, 249B East Thirty-Fifth Street is an ordinary brownstone, but with so many rooms and corridors upstairs, a person could get lost.

Black House: Standing outside, one sees a dark three-story dwelling. Upon going inside, one is confronted with an enormous circular foyer with numerous doors and countless stairways. Some rooms are bigger than the house itself.

The Dark Tower: When you wake up inside the Little Sisters' hospital tent, you see a bright white expanse. If you get the rare chance to exit, you'll find only a plain tent.

Killer Tanker Trucks

Pet Sematary: Gage Creed found a new game: run away from his parents. He ran onto Route 15, in front of an Orinco truck. A senseless tragedy.

The Tommyknockers: Hilly Brown flew on his Flexible Flyer sled down his frozen driveway, heading toward the street where a Webber Fuel tanker approached. He fell off the sled and broke his left arm when his mother screamed. The trucker ran into a ditch to avoid the sled he didn't know was empty.

Elsa Lanchester Hair

Elsa Lanchester hair means a style resembling that of Elsa Lanchester's character in Bride of Frankenstein. It's not flattering.

"The Mist": Mrs. Carmody

"In the Deathroom": a woman on the deathroom tribunal interrogating Fletcher

11/22/63: Alberta Hitchinson, the woman with a walker who had a neighbor call an ambulance for George Amberson

Mr. Mercedes: Mrs. Elizabeth Wharton's home-care nurse, Mrs. Althea Greene

the Land of Ago

Bag of Bones: Mike Noonan referred to the past as the Land of Ago.

11/22/63: Jake Epping traveled back in time and lived as George Amberson in the Land of Ago.

the Ludlow House

Pet Sematary: The Creeds lived in a white New England Colonial on Route 15 in Ludlow, ME.

The Dark Half: So did the Beaumonts, but none of the neighbors in *The Dark Half* were mentioned in *Pet Sematary* or vice versa. Also, we don't know whether Louis and Ellie Creed moved.

Monsters

the setup:

> *'Salem's Lot*: Vampire Danny Glick scratched outside Mark Petrie's window.
>
> "Gray Matter": George Kelso saw a dog-sized spider in the sewers under Bangor, ME.
>
> *Cujo*: Tad Trenton feared a monster in his closet. His father's nightly recitation of THE MONSTER WORDS kept Tad safe.

the Easter Eggs:

> *IT*: 1) Ben Hanscom thought, "[y]ou no longer lay awake in your bed, sure something was crouching in your closet or scratching at the window . . ." 2) IT existed in the form of a large spider under Derry's sewers.

moving hedge animals

The Shining: The grounds of the Overlook Hotel included a topiary garden. Throughout the winter, Danny Torrance and his father, Jack, each saw that the animals had moved.

Billy Summers: Billy Summers wrote in the summerhouse behind Bucky Hanson's place in Sidewinder, CO. A picture of hedge animals hung on the wall. Billy swore the animals had moved from time to time.

Murderers With Iron-Tight Alibis

The Dark Half: Fingerprint and other evidence pointed to Thad Beaumont as a killer, but he had a wonderful alibi.

The Outsider: Iron-clad evidence showed Terry Maitland a killer; a cast-iron alibi suggested he wasn't.

Number One Fan

Misery: Annie Wilkes proclaimed herself Paul Sheldon's Number One Fan.

Insomnia: Lois Roberts told Connie Chung she was her number one fan.

Finders Keepers: Morris Bellamy was John Rothstein's number one fan until he felt Rothstein sold out.

Old Sparky

the nickname of prison electric chairs

"The Jaunt": Florida

> —Rudy Foggia, destined for Old Sparky, accepted the offer of being a human subject to test Jaunt travel.

The Dark Tower, "My Pretty Pony": Sing Sing's electric chair

The Green Mile:

> —Arlen Bitterbuck, Tillman Clark, John Coffey, Eduard Delacroix, Elmer Manfred, Anthony Ray were executed on Old Sparky in Cold Mountain Penitentiary.

Out-of-This-World Pregnant Critters

IT: IT

Dreamcatcher: the byrum at Hole in the Wall

From a Buick 8: the bat-thing from the Buick

Owen Teddy Bears

Note: Owen is the name of the Kings' younger son.

Christine: Kenny Guilder made toys. The bears he always named Owen and Olive.

Needful Things: Tansy Williams had a teddy bear named Owen.

Pictures that change

Rose Madder: Rosie McClendon picked up a painting of Rose Madder when she started her new life. Although the overall dimensions remained the same, the picture grew in that the viewer could see more and more within it as time went on.

"The Road Virus Heads North": Heading home to Derry after a conference in Boston, Richard Kinnell bought a painting at a yard sale. As Richard drove home, the painting's scenery changed to show Road Virus—the car in the painting—following him home.

Billy Summers: Billy wrote in the summerhouse behind Bucky Hanson's place near Sidewinder, CO. Each time he looked at a painting of topiary animals, he swore the animals had moved.

Plymouth Fury, white-over-red

Christine: Roland D. LeBay sold Christine, a 1958 Plymouth Fury, to Arnie Cunningham.

11/22/63: Jake Epping saw a white-over-red Plymouth Fury in the Worumbo Mills & Weaving parking lot.

Psi Powers for Assassination

"Everything's Eventual": Trans Corporation recruited people with the trans trait (those who exhibited postcognition, precognition, pkyrokinesis, telempathy, telepathy, etc.) to cause those they deemed undesirable to commit suicide.

The Institute: The Institute abducted telepathic and telekinetic children to band together to cause accidental deaths of people they thought the world would be better without.

Psychic Substances

The Dark Tower: The Wolves took one of each pair of twins to extract the secretion that created twin telepathy.

Doctor Sleep: Psychically inclined children had a tasty steam, which, unfortunately, was enhanced by extreme and extensive pain.

The Institute: TK (telekinetic) and TP (telepathic) children had higher levels of Brain-Derived Neurotrophic Factor (BDNF) levels than lay people.

Rainbird

Firestarter: John Rainbird was a prominent baddie.

The Talisman: Rainbird Towers, a condominium under construction, collapsed in an earthquake when Jack Sawyer flipped between worlds.

Separation of Mind and Body

Dreamcatcher: Henry's and Duddits's bodies slept as their minds were in the dreamcatcher.

The Dark Tower: Bodies remained behind when people went todash.

Sleeping Beauties: The bodies of Wheeling, WV's women stayed behind while their minds lived on the other side of the Tree.

the Shine

Clairvoyant people who could communicate telepathically had the shine, also known as the shining.

The Shining: Dick Hallorann and Danny Torrance had the shine.

The Stand: Mother Abagail had prophetic dreams. Her grandmother called her prophecy the shine.

Pet Sematary: Jud Crandall had the knack for knowing what Louis Creed was thinking. Could we call that a shine?

Sonny's Gas Stations

'Salem's Lot: Sonny James ran Sonny's Amoco-Exxon on Jointner Avenue in Jerusalem's Lot.

"The Body": Castle Rock had a Sonny's Texaco.

"The Sun Dog": Sonny Jackett ran Sonny's Texaco in Castle Rock.

Needful Things: Sonny Jackett ran Sonny's Sunoco in Castle Rock.

"Home Delivery": Sonny Dotson ran Island Amoco on Jenny Island.

The Colorado Kid: Sonny's Sunoco on Moose-Lookit Island

Cell: Sonny's Texaco in Malden Center in Malden, MA

"Drunken Fireworks": Sonny's Garage in Castle County

Spare Keys in Sucrets Tins

"Apt Pupil": Todd Bowden said a safe deposit box key could easily be hidden in a Sucrets tin.

Bag of Bones: The Noonans kept a spare key to their summer home in a Sucrets tin under the deck.

"The Gingerbread Girl": Emily Owensby's father kept a spare key to his conch shack in a Sucrets tin under a garden gnome.

11/22/63: George Amberson found the key to a 1954 Ford Sunliner in a Sucrets tin in the glovebox.

Tommyknockers

The Tommyknockers: space travelers alien to Earth

Desperation: underground troublemaking gremlins

Town Barriers

The Tommyknockers: The Haven Tommyknockers built an invisible, impenetrable barrier at the edge of town, a flexible, rubbery barrier.

Under the Dome: Alien leatherheads generated a similar, but rigid, barrier around Chester's Mill.

Word Replacement

"The Moving Finger": Howard Mitla found himself using the word "finger" instead of similar-sounding words in ordinary conversation ("finger" for "fever," for example).

"Rat": Drew Larson heard "rat" from others in conversation (e.g., "rat" for "rash").

Joe Hill Connections and Easter Eggs

Connections and Easter Eggs from Stephen King to Joe Hill

Doctor Sleep: Grampa Andy threatened to have Charlie Manx take Dickie Hallorann away if Dickie told about Grampa Andy's assaults. (Charlie Manx is the antagonist in Joe Hill's *NOS4A2*.)

Doctor Sleep: The True Knot had a "I HELPED TRIM THE WORLD'S BIGGEST TREE IN CHRISTMASLAND" bumper sticker on an RV. (Christmasland is a Charlie Manx inscape.)

Mr. Mercedes: A roadie in a Judas Coyne T-shirt helped Bill Hodges until EMTs arrived. (Judas Coyne was the main character of Joe Hill's *Heart-Shaped Box*.)

[**Easter Egg**] "Mile 81": Pete Simmons had the latest issue of *Locke & Key*.

Connections and Easter Eggs from Joe Hill to Stephen King

[**Easter Egg**] *Locke and Key*: "They have the new Buick 8 . . ." (Stephen King's *From a Buick 8*)

[**Easter Egg**] *Locke and Key*: "Nothing smells better than a new car . . . except maybe for Toronto pussy." (Stephen King's Roland LeBay had similar sentiments about that particular female attraction, but not necessarily one from Toronto.)

Locke and Key: the Children of Leng (Stephen King's *The Eyes of the Dragon* and *Needful Things* had the Plains of Leng.)

[**Easter Egg**] *Horns*: ". . . soaked in poultry blood like the chick in . . . *Carrie*."

Horns: Glenna Nicholson's uncle ran a used auto parts business in Derry.

[**Easter Egg**] "Wolverton Station": "[I]t made him look like Jack Nicholson with the ax in that movie." (That movie being *The Shining*, of course.)

NOS4A2: Pennywise Circus was an inscape near Derry, ME.

NOS4A2: A guy ran Transcendental Meditation therapy for Shawshank prisoners with anger-management issues.

NOS4A2: Charlie Manx knew of doors to Mid-World.

NOS4A2: Charlie Manx and the True Knot left each other alone.

[**Easter Egg**] *NOS4A2*: Bing Partridge to Charlie Manx: "My life! For you!" (This is like the Trashcan Man's "My life for you!" to Randall Flagg/The Ageless Stranger in *The Stand* and *The Dark Tower*.)

NOS4A2: Maggie Leigh went to the Nite Owl in Here, IA, for ramen noodles.

[**Easter Egg**] *The Fireman*: "They had forgotten their own names, the voices of their mothers, the faces of their fathers." (*The Dark Tower*'s Roland was disgusted with people who had forgotten the faces of their fathers.)

[**Easter Egg**] *The Fireman*: "The aspiring novelist in me wants a secret tunnel hidden behind . . . a poster of a famous movie star." (the pinup posters in "Rita Hayworth and Shawshank Redemption")

The Fireman: When Harper and the others were hiding out at the South Street Cemetery, the Fireman brought a cart of food and Nozz-A-La cola.

[Easter Egg] “Snapshot”: “. . . so she could listen to the soundtrack of *Stand By Me*” (the movie)

Basketful of Heads: Four members of a Shawshank Prison (in Derry County, ME) work-detail escaped.

Appendix 1: Fictional Towns

I know what you're thinking. Did he write six fictional towns or only five? In all the excitement of reading Stephen King over the years, I kind of lost track myself. It turns out, there's more, mmmm, lots more:

Fictional Towns in Maine

Apex, ME

Blaze: Blaze lived in a shack in Apex.

Bankerton, ME

Thinner: Richard Ginelli fired a Kalishnikov AK-47 automatic assault rifle over the Gypsies' heads at their camp in Bankerton.

Big Tall Island, ME

Storm of the Century: one of Maine's Outer Islands

Cashman, ME

11/22/63: Frank Dunning and his first wife lived near the Cashman town line.

Castle Rock, ME

See the Locale Connections chapter.

Chamberlain, ME

See the Locale Connections chapter.

Cleaves Mills, ME

See the Locale Connections chapter.

Dark Score Lake in Maine

See the Locale Connections chapter.

Dawson, ME

11/22/63: George Amberson set his novel, *The Murder Place*, in Dawson, modeled after Derry.

Dennison River Bend, ME

The Institute: This was the nearest down to the Institute's compound in TR–110.

Derry, ME

See the Locale Connections chapter.

Dowrie, ME

"Mute": Barb Monette worked and had an affair in Dowrie.

Gardener, ME

Pet Sematary: Alan Purinton was a Ludlow resident in Timmy Baterman's day, then lived in a nursing home up in Gardener.

Gates Falls, ME

See the Locale Connections chapter.

Gennesault (Jenny) Island, ME

"Home Delivery": Zombies struck Jenny Island.

Goat Island, ME

"Do the Dead Sing?" / "The Reach": The story is set on Goat Island.

Gretna, ME

See the Locale Connections chapter.

Gurleyville, ME, an unincorporated township

Cell: Ray Huizenga loaded a school bus with explosives from the Gurleyville Quarry.

Haven, ME

See the Locale Connections chapter.

Harlow and South Harlow, ME

See the Locale Connections chapter.

Jerusalem's Lot, ME

See the Locale Connections chapter.

Kankamongus Island, ME

Storm of the Century: one of Maine's Outer Islands

Kashwakamak Township (Kashwak), ME

See the Locale Connections chapter.

Kashwakamak Lake in Maine

See the Locale Connections chapter.

Kent Pond, ME

Cell: Clay Riddell lived in Kent Pond.

Kewadin/Keywadin Pond in Maine

See the Locale Connections chapter.

Kineo, ME

Dreamcatcher: Rick McCarthy and three others hunted around Kineo in Maine's Jefferson Tract.

Little Tall Island, ME

See the Locale Connections chapter.

Ludlow, ME

See the Locale Connections chapter.

Mile 81 Rest Area on the Maine Turnpike (I-95)

See the Locale Connections chapter.

Moose-Lookit Island, ME

The Colorado Kid: Two teens found James Cogan (aka the Colorado Kid) dead on the beach of Moose-Lookit Island.

Motton, ME

See the Locale Connections chapter.

Nodd's Ridge, ME

Tabitha King's fictional town

Needful Things: Nodd's Ridge was a logging town near Castle Lake.

Ocoma Heights, ME

Blaze: The Gerards lived in Ocoma Heights. Blaze kidnapped Joseph Gerard IV.

Placerville, ME

Rage: Charlie Decker held a class of kids at the High School.

Porterville, ME

The Long Walk: Ray Garraty's hometown

Raccoon Head, ME

"Do the Dead Sing?"/"The Reach": A drunken George Dinsmore ran a snowplow through three utility poles in this town across the Reach from Goat Island.

Shaymore, ME

"The Mist": The Arrowhead Project hailed from Shaymore.

Smack Island, ME

The Colorado Kid: In 1927, the *Pretty Lisa Cabot* washed up on Smack Island, near Moose-Lookit Island. The mystery of all ten crewmen being dead or missing remains unsolved.

St. Christopher, ME

"Rat": St. Christopher, the closest town to Drew Larson's cabin in TR–90, was forty-five miles away.

St. Ives and Castle-St. Ives, ME

"N.": Amateur photographer N. took pictures in these and other towns along the Androscoggin River.

Tarker's Mills, ME

See the Locale Connections chapter.

Tashmore Glen (Tashmore) and Tashmore Pond, ME

See the Locale Connections chapter.

Tecknor, ME

Thinner: Billy Halleck found the Gypsies on a rented field in Tecknor. Gina Lemke shot a steel ball bearing through his left hand.

Tinnock Village (Tinnock), ME

The Colorado Kid: Tinnock Village was across the reach from Moose-Lookit Island.

TR-90, ME

See the Locale Connections chapter.

TR-100, ME

See the Locale Connections chapter.

TR-110, ME

See the Locale Connections chapter.

Westover, ME

Carrie: Harold Kuebler pronounced Carrie DOA at Westover Mercy Hospital in Westover, a town near Chamberlain.

Willow, ME

"Rainy Season": Every seven years, it rained toads in Willow. Residents knew to stay indoors and batten down the hatches. Outsiders snickered at warnings to stay out of town for the night. The toads killed them, and Willow prospered for another seven years.

Fictional Towns Outside Maine

Alderton, NY

"The Night Flier": The Night Flier killed Buck Kendall at Lakeview Airport in Alderton.

Anniston, NH

Doctor Sleep: Abra Stone lived in Anniston.

Arcadia Beach, NH

See the Locale Connections chapter.

Arden, WI

Black House: Judy Marshall stayed at the French County Lutheran Hospital in Arden, near French Landing.

Arnette, TX

See the Locale Connections chapter.

Aubreyville

Rose Madder: Rose McClendon and Norman Daniels were from Aubreyville. They may or may not have moved after they married.

Aynesford, MA

IT: A body found in a gravel-pit here was not Eddie Corcoran's.

Babylon, AL

The Plant: Riddley Walker's Aunt Olympia lived in Babylon.

Bakersville, Colorado

American Vampire: Skinner Sweet and his gang robbed a bank in Bakersville and got away with a mining company's payroll of almost $20,000.

Bankerton, IA

Doctor Sleep: Steamhead Bradley Trevor lived on a farm in Bankerton.

Belwood District, California

"In a Half-World of Terror": Steffen Weinbaum experimented with dead flesh in the Belwood District.

Beson, DE

Squad D's Jimmy Oliphant was from Beson.

Bitter River, Wyoming

"Rat": Drew Larson's *Bitter River* was set in 1880s Bitter River, Wyoming.

Black Fork, Arizona

The Dark Tower: Calvin Tower mentioned this hypothetical Old West town.

Blackwater, AL

The Plant: Riddley Walker's mother lived and died in Blackwater.

Blessington, UT

The Talisman: Every November, Randy Glover, Phil Sawyer, Morgan Sloat, and Tommy Woodbine stayed at Randy's hunting lodge in Blessington. Morgan Sloat had Sunlight Gardener/Osmond kill Sawyer; Sloat reported Phil Sawyer died in a hunting accident.

Braintree, TX

The Stand: Joe Bob Brentwood passed Captain Trips to Harry Trent, an insurance salesman from Braintree, while giving him a speeding ticket. Harry Trent infected the Edward Norris family at Babe's Kwik-Eat. Braintree neighbors Arnette.

Burrack, AZ

The Stand: Poke Freeman and Lloyd Henreid killed a couple of folks inside Pop's, a café/store/gas station in Burrack. Arizona State Police apprehended him outside and took him to the Apache County Jail in Phoenix.

Cabral, CA

Firestarter: Vicky Tomlinson's best friend in the first grade grew up to be Mrs. Frank Worthy, living in Cabral.

Candy, KS

"All That You Love Will Be Carried Away": Alfie Zimmer collected graffiti from a rest area on Route 283 in Candy.

Canning Township, OK

The Outsider: After being Terry Maitland, the outsider hung out in a disused barn near the abandoned Cowboy Graveyard.

Cap City, OK

The Outsider: Terry Maitland was attending a teacher's conference in Cap City at the same time he was brutalizing a boy in Flint City.

Capital City, NH

The Dead Zone: A girl wanted Greg Stillson's autograph at a campaign rally in Capital City. His security gave her a dislocated neck and a broken arm instead.

Caymen Key, FL

"Laurie": Widower Lloyd Sunderland and his dog, Laurie, met an alligator on their way to lunch.

Centralia, WI

Black House: The Thunder Five hung out at the Sand Bar in Centralia.

Colewich Township and North Colewich, MA

"Big Driver": Big Driver and his brother, Lester Strehlke, lived and died in Colewich Township.

Columbia City, OH

"Everything's Eventual": Dinky Earnshaw lived in Columbia City while he worked for TransCorp, sending fatal letters to those the company deemed undesirable.

Coorter's Notch, NH

The Dead Zone: Greg Stillson held a Feedback Center in Coorter's Notch.

Coose Lake, NY

The Dead Zone: Stanbury Richards, Dr. Vann's brother-in-law, fell from a ladder and broke his back while painting. A week before, Johnny Smith thought Strawberry had been hurt; Dr. Vann's son called Stanbury "Uncle Strawberry."

Crowheart Springs, WY

"Willa": An Amtrak train derailed in Wyoming. For about twenty years, the victims' ghosts waited in a condemned railway station for Amtrak to send another train.

Crownville, NY

Doctor Sleep: After Crow Daddy was taken care of, Billy Freeman and Abra Stone slept in adjoining rooms at the Crown Motel.

Coughlin, WV

Sleeping Beauties: Lila Norcross saw a girl with the unfortunate name of Sheila Norcross play basketball in Coughlin. Life between Lila and Clint Norcross changed forever.

Cumba, AZ

"Throttle": After overhearing that the Tribe had killed his daughter, Laughlin ran down several motorcycle club members near this old mining town.

Cutlersville, NY

The Plant: General Hecksler escaped from the Oak Cove Asylum in Cutlersville.

Dead River

"Old Chief Wood'nhead" (Creepshow 2): Old Chief Wood'nhead stood outside Spruce's General Store for over sixty years.

Dead Steer Springs

"Slade": Jack Slade helped Sandra Dawson deal with Sam Columbine. And then he dealt with her.

Dead Wolf, MT

"Rest Stop": John Dykstra imagined a movie about a paranoid missile-silo commander in some out-of-the-way area such as Dead Wolf, MT, or Lonesome Crow, ND.

Deadwood Gulch, AZ

Black House: the setting of Lily Cavanaugh's 1950 film *The Terror of Deadwood Gulch*

Deland, NE

"1922": The Farrington Company had offices in Deland.

Dellacourt, MS

"Secret Window, Secret Garden": John Shooter was a Dellacourt dairy farmer.

Derbyshire, TN

The Stand: The Free Zone's doctor, George Richardson, was from Derbyshire.

Desperation, NV

Desperation: China Pit mine blasting freed Tak.

Devon Township, PA

“Big Wheels: A Tale of the Laundry Game”: Devon Stream separated Crescent Township and Devon Township.

Dooling, WV

Sleeping Beauties: Supernatural misandrist Evie Black visited Dooling.

Dry Bend, NM

Doctor Sleep: a True Not “company town” and safe haven

Dubrow, OK

The Outsider: The Vogel Transportation Center, a major hub in southern Oklahoma, was in Dubrow.

Duffrey, MD

“The Night Flier”: The Night Flier killed Ellen and Ray Sarch, who ran Duffrey Airfield.

Duma Key, FL

Duma Key: After nearly dying in an accident with a crane, Edgar Freemantle started a new life in Duma Key.

Dunbrie, MS

Doctor Sleep: Dick Hallorann’s evil grandfather lived in Dunbrie.

Dunning, SC

The Institute: Dunning had a gun range and an agricultural fair.

Dunwich, MA

"The Sun Dog": A Mad Hatter became insane at the Dunwich Cemetery in Dunwich.

Note: Dunwich, MA, is the town from H. P. Lovecraft's "The Dunwich Horror."

DuPray, SC

The Institute: Luke Ellis's and Tim Jamieson's lives collided in this small Fairlee County town.

Durban, IL

Firestarter: The Shop planned to send Andy McGee to the Maui compound. The plane would refuel in Durban.

East Conway Village, NH

The Dark Tower: A walk-in died in East Conway Village.

Edendale, TN

Billy Summers: Darlene Summers, Billy's mom, worked at 24 Hour Laundry in Edendale.

Eustace, OK

The Stand: The Edward Norris family infected a travel-court clerk and other guests in Eustace.

Everytown, PA

"The Hitch-Hiker" (*Creepshow 2*): Annie Lansing hit a hitch-hiker on her way home. She was heading to Everyville; he was going to Harrisburg.

Fabyan, NH

The Stand: Stu Redman met Fran Goldsmith and Harold Lauder on US 302 in Fabyan.

Fanning, Arizona

American Vampire: Pinkerton Special Agent James Book captured Butch Yeager and his gang in 1885 Fanning.

Fairview, CT

Thinner: The Halleck family lived in Fairview.

Fenderville, VT

The Talisman: Jack Sawyer used the alias Jack Sawtelle, from Fenderville.

Fields, VA

Finders Keepers: Bill Hodges told Oliver Madden they arrested Madden's brother-in-law in Fields, VA. They didn't.

Flint City, OK

See the Locale Connections chapter.

Freeman, IA

Doctor Sleep: Rose the Hat tortured Bradley Trevor behind a defunct ethanol plant in Freeman to purify his steam. He lasted a long time.

French Landing, WI

See the Locale Connections chapter.

Gaiten, NH

Cell: Alice Maxwell, Tom McCourt, and Clay Riddell stayed awhile at Gaiten Academy. Jordan joined them when they moved on.

Gatlin, NE

See the Locale Connections chapter.

Gaylord, MO

Dolores Claiborne: Vera Donovan was born in Gaylord.

Glen's Falls, NH

Cell: Normies burned a flock of phone-crazies in Glen's Falls or Littleton.

Glointon, NY

IT: Patricia Uris, Stan's wife, was from Glointon.

Glory, WV

Christine: Veronica LeBay's brother lived here.

Goslin, OH

The Talisman: Mr. Buddy Parkins, of Goslin, gave Lewis Farren (Jack Sawyer) a ride from Cambridge, OH, to Zanesville.

Gowanda, PA

Finders Keepers: Morris Bellamy ran his car through a carwash in Gowanda. He had just run over Curtis Rogers at a rest stop in upstate New York.

Grainger, WI

Black House: A few men beat up Merlin Graasheimer in Grainger because they thought he might have been the Fisherman.

Great Bluff, Wisconsin

Black House: In 1888, Far Eyes, chief of the Fox Indian tribe, had his people commit suicide by jumping off a limestone outcropping at Great Bluff.

Greeno, CT

Thinner: They Gypsies were rousted from Greeno.

Hadley

The Cannibals (unpublished): Tennis Club Apartments resident Pamela Andeyric ran an accounting business in Hadley.

Hammersmith, OH

Firestarter: After Andy McGee rescued Charlie McGee from Shop agents at a turnpike rest area, Andy and Charlie spent the night at a Best Western in Hammersmith.

Harkerville, PA

"Everything's Eventual": Dinky Earnshaw grew up in Harkerville.

Harko, IL

Black House: Thunder Five member Sonny Cantinaro found Harko to be a bad place. Real bad.

Harwich, CT

See the Locale Connections chapter.

Hastings Glen, NY

Firestarter: Charlie McGee caused a ruckus with Shop agents at the Manders farm in Hastings Glen.

the Hauck ghetto in Cleveland

The Dark Tower: Joe Collins (Dandelo) performed at Jango's. (Or did he?)

Hayes Station, NH

Cell: Clay Riddell's group stayed at the Whispering Pines motel.

Heaven's Bay, NC

Joyland: Devin Jones got a summer job at Joyland Amusement Park in Heaven's Bay.

Hemingford City, NE

"1922": twenty miles from Hemingford Home

Hemingford Home, NE

See the Locale Connections chapter.

Ink Beach, FL

Misery: Ink Beach resident Virginia Sandpiper turned an upstairs room into a replica of Misery's Parlor.

Jamesburg

Christine: Arnie Cunningham ran auto parts to Jamesburg for Will Darnell.

Jodie, TX

11/22/63: George Amberson hung out as a high school teacher in Jodie while he waited for Lee Harvey Oswald.

Jubilee, KS

"All That You Love Will Be Carried Away": Alfie Zimmer may have purchased the spiral notebook he collected graffiti with in a Jubilee five-and-dime.

Junction City, IA

See the Locale Connections chapter.

Junkins, NE

IT: The adult Ben Hanscom lived on a farm in Junkins, near Gatlin and Hemingford Home.

Key Caroline, FL

"I Am the Doorway": Arthur moved to Key Caroline after his Venus trip.

Lake Belle Reve, Darkland County, MS

Ghost Brothers of Darkland County: Tragedy struck the McCandless family twice, forty years apart.

Lakeview, Colorado

American Vampire: Because Bram Percy's dam flooded Sidewinder, Colorado, Mrs. Pruitt moved her Boarding House to Lakeview.

La Riviere, WI

Black House: Reporter Wendell Green was from this town bordering French Landing.

Lassburg, PA

From a Buick 8: a town near Statler Township

Latchmore, NY

Revival: Charlie Jacobs continued his secret electricity research in a lab on a sprawling gated estate in Latchmore.

Le Dio, SC

"The Body": A young Gordie Lachance wrote many World War II stories set in Le Dio.

the Plains of Leng

See the Locale Connections chapter.

Lewis, SC

The Stand: Rebecca and John Freemantle were slaves under Sam Freemantle in Lewis.

Libertyville, PA

Christine: Arnie Cunningham fell in love with Christine in Libertyville.

Lonesome Crow, ND

"Rest Stop": John Dykstra imagined a movie about a paranoid missile-silo commander in some out-of-the-way area such as Dead Wolf, MT, or Lonesome Crow, ND.

Longmont, VA

Firestarter: The Shop's primary compound was in Longmont. Cap Hollister lived in Longmont Hills.

Los Zapatos, Mexico

See the Locale Connections chapter.

Lovinger, NY

"Keyholes": Michael Briggs lived in Lovinger, forty miles north of New York City.

the City of Lud

See the Locale Connections chapter.

Lyme Biska, NE

"1922": 1) A skeleton found near Lyme Biska was assumed to have been that of Arlette James after she had supposedly run off. 2) Henry James robbed a grocery-ethyl station of $23.

Maidstone, NH

"Mr. Harrigan's Phone": Drunk driver Dean Whitmore didn't last long at the Raven Mountain Treatment Center.

Marathon, PA

The Stand: Lloyd Henreid grew up in Marathon.

Martensburg, PA

Lisey's Story: Scott Landon grew up in this western rural Pennsylvania town.

Martenville, CO

Doctor Sleep: To fool the True Knot into thinking Abra Stone was at their campground, Dan Torrance bought a mannequin and children's clothes at Kids' Stuff.

Maylock, WV

Sleeping Beauties: the next town over from Dooling

Mayville, TN

Billy Summers: Billy Summers grew up in Mayville.

Miller, WI

Black House: a town near French Landing

Mink Crossing, WV

Sleeping Beauties: Dispatcher Linny Mars was from Kanawha County, so she could understand people talking with the local accent.

Moore, KY

"Ur": With a special Kindle, Wesley Smith annoyed low men in yellow coats.

Morgan, IL

"The Wedding Gig": Tommy Englander ran a speakeasy near this town outside Chicago.

Murfreesboro, GA

The Stand: While picking blackberries, Sam Tauber fell in a well, broke both legs, and died the next morning.

Nestor Falls, MA

"Big Driver": a town near Colewich Township

Norris County, Colorado

Revival: Evangelist C. Danny Jacobs healed people of their afflictions during revival shows at the Norris County Fairgrounds.

Northport, CT

Thinner: Billy Halleck moved to Northport when he was a teenager.

Norway Valley, WI

Black House: Jack Sawyer bought Dale Gilbertson's father's house outside French Landing.

Oatley, NY

See the Locale Connections chapter.

Oree, FL

Doctor Sleep: a True Not "company town" and safe haven

Paiute, NV

Billy Summers: Nick Majarian lived in this town north of Las Vegas.

Paradise Falls, OH

See the Locale Connections chapter.

Patchin, PA

From a Buick 8: Huddie Royer assisted at a three-car accident scene involving a drunk driver in this town near Statler Township.

Patin concentration camp

"Apt Pupil": Kurt Dussander was the Blood-Fiend of Patin.

Payson, ND

Squad D member Charlie Gibson was from Payson.

Peakville, Colorado

American Vampire: The Peakville *Envoy* was the local paper.

Penley, SC

The Institute: The strip club in this town neighboring DuPray had closed.

Penniston, NY

"Stationary Bike": Penniston fell between Poughkeepsie and Herkimer on Richard Sifkitz's imaginary bike rides.

Perkinsburg, MS

"Secret Window, Secret Garden": John Shooter bought a copy of Morton Rainey's *Everybody Drops the Dime* in Perkinsburg. He was incensed to find that Morton had plagiarized his "Secret Window, Secret Garden" as Mort's own "Sowing Season."

Pierre Village, PA

"If It Bleeds": The World's Largest Garage Sale was held in Pierre Village.

Pineborough Township, PA

"If It Bleeds": Psychic vampire Chet Ondowsky delivered a bomb to the Albert Macready Middle School.

Placer's Glen, CT

"The Cat From Hell": After the deaths of three companions involving Sam, Drogan hired hit-man John Halston to sanction the cat. Sam killed Halston outside Placer's Glen.

Plainville, TX

The Outsider: Holly Gibney, Ralph Anderson, and others flew into Plainville before meeting the outsider.

Pogus City, PA

From a Buick 8: a town near Statler Township

Point Venuti, CA

The Talisman: The Agincourt Hotel was in Point Venuti. The Black Hotel stood at its corresponding location in the Territories.

Polliston, KS

The Stand: Sarah Bradford, of Polliston, caught Captain Trips from the Ed Norris family when she paid her bill at Dr. Sweeney's office. She went on to infect her family, bridge club, and cocktail bar patrons.

Port City, PA

Firestarter: Andy McGee ran a Weight-Off program in Port City.

Poteenville, PA

From a Buick 8: A tanker-truck and a school bus collided on County Road 46.

Powtanville, IN

The Stand: In his hometown of Powtanville, IN, Donald Merwin Elbert picked up the nickname The Trashcan Man for setting fires in neighbors' garbage cans.

Preacher's Corners, ME

"Jerusalem's Lot": a town near the deserted village of Jerusalem's Lot

Pretty Nice, NV

Desperation: Johnny Marinville gassed up his Harley in Pretty Nice.

Proverbia, IA

"The Library Policeman": neighbored Junction City

Province, VT

"The Jaunt": The Jaunt was tested with human subjects in Province.

Raintree, CT

Thinner: Taduz Lemke cursed Cary Rossington at a flea market in Raintree.

Red Bluff, AR

Billy Summers: Hitman Billy Summers traveled to Red Bluff for his last hit before retiring.

Redmont Hills, PA

Hearts in Atlantis: The adult Bobby Garfield lived in Redmont Hills, near Philadelphia.

Reedville, PA

Lisey's Story: Reedville had a nutbarn (a mental hospital).

Regis, OH

The Outsider: Heath Holmes visited his mother in Regis, OH, at the same time he killed the Howard girls in Trotwood.

Renfield, NY

Later: Drug kingpin Donnie Marsden lived in Renfield. Liz Dutton wanted Jamie Conklin to help find his stash after he died.

Ridgeway, NH

The Dead Zone: Greg Stillson was the mayor of Ridgeway.

River City

The Cannibals (unpublished): Tennis Club Apartments residents couldn't get out of the building one morning.

Roaring Rock, Wyoming

The Stand: Roberta Anderson set *Rimfire Christmas* in Roaring Rock.

Rock and Roll Heaven, OR

"You Know They Got a Hell of a Band": Dead rock-and-rollers performed endless concerts nightly.

Rocksburg, PA

See the Locale Connections chapter.

Rome, NH

Lisey's Story: A month before they married, Lisey Debusher and Scott Landon went to the Antlers in Rome, NH, on a frontloaded honeymoon.

Round Hill, TX

11/22/63: George Amberson and Sadie Dunhill liked to eat at The Saddle in Round Hill.

San Remo, CA

"Apt Pupil": Victor S Bowden, Todd's grandfather, lived at 403 Ridge Lane, San Remo.

Santa Mira, CA

The Dark Tower: The group that recruited Breakers drove Ted Brautigan and others to Santa Mira to go through a door to Thunderclap Station.

Santo Donato, CA

"Apt Pupil": Todd Bowden and Arthur Denker lived and killed in Santo Donato.

Schubert, WI

Black House: a town near French Landing

Sedonville, CT

The Dark Tower: Truman Alexander and 'Cimi Dretto buried an Irish man under a chicken house in Sedonville. Balazar had shot him in the head for blowing down Balazar's house of cards.

Shabene, PA

From a Buick 8: Shabene had a prison.

Shooter's Knob, TN

See the Locale Connections chapter.

Shoshone, CO

The Stand: Between snow storms, Tom Cullen, Kojak, and Stu Redman passed through Shoshone.

Shoyo, AR

The Stand: Thugs beat up Nick Andros in Shoyo. Sheriff John Baker took him in.

Sidewinder, CO

See the Locale Connections chapter.

South Gansett, NH

"A Good Marriage": Marjorie Duvall, Beadie's last victim, lived in South Gansett.

South Ryegate, NH

The Stand: Glen Bateman met Stu Redman on US 302, near South Ryegate.

Spofford, OH

The Dark Tower: Donald Callahan was a priest in Spofford for five years.

Spuytenkill, NY

The Outsider: The outsider's dirty white van belonged to Carl Jellison of Spuytenkill, a town between New Paltz and Poughkeepsie.

Statesboro, PA

From a Buick 8: had a Comedy Shop

Statler Township, PA

From a Buick 8: An out-of-this-world Buick Roadmaster showed up in Statler. Troop D kept it in Shed B.

Stoke Village, CT

"Big Driver": Tessa Jean, author of *the Willow Grove Knitting Society* mysteries, lived here.

Storyville, OH

Pet Sematary: The American Casket Company of Storyville made Gage Creed's Eternal Rest casket.

Storyville, CA

The Talisman: Wolf's brother Wolf picked up Jack Sawyer and Richard Sloat at a Mobil station in Storyville and drove them across the country.

Stovington, VT

See the Locale Connections chapter.

Talbot, AL

"Bad Little Kid": The bad little kid caused the death of Marlee Jacobs.

Talbot Corners, NH

Finders Keepers: John Rothstein kept to himself on a farm in Talbot Corners.

Tassel Village, MA

"A Good Marriage": Beadie victims Helen Shaverstone and her ten-year-old son, Robert, lived here. They were found dumped in a creek twelve miles away.

Tashmore, VT

Firestarter: Charlie and Andy McGee holed up at Granther's place in Tashmore. They didn't know the Shop watched them for five months before sending Rainbird to round them up.

Teller, NH

Firestarter: Shop agent Charles Payson saw Andy McGee mail letters in Bradford, NH. The Teller post office served Bradford and Williams, NH. Shop agents rudely took Andy's letters from postman Robert Everett.

Thumper, FL

"Home Delivery": The first reports of zombies in America were from Thumper. *Inside View* got the scoop.

Tilton, VT

"*The New York Times* at Special Bargain Rates": Anne and James Driscoll sold their Tilton summer cottage ten years ago.

Tippit, TX

The Outsider: Claude Bolton drove to Highway Heaven in Tippit, forty miles from Marysville, for chicken dinners.

Titusville, AR

"The Little Green God of Agony": A wildfire started by drunken campers destroyed The Church of Holy Faith, Reverend Rideout's church.

Titusville, IN

"The House on Maple Street": The Bradbury's house on Maple Street grew a rocket and blasted off.

Traynor, GA

IT: Before Atlanta, Patricia and Stan Uris lived in Traynor.

Timmesdale, NH

The Dead Zone: Dick O'Donnell ran the Timmesdale Pub. Over beers at the Pub, Johnny Smith learned Greg Stillson held revolving town hall meetings in New Hampshire. Jackson, NH, was next.

Trimbull, NH

The Dead Zone: Johnny Smith foresaw Greg Stillson start World War III when he shook Stillson's hand at a campaign rally in Trimbull. He woke up in a jail cell.

Twickenham, MA

Cujo: Massachusetts State Police picked up Steve Kemp in Twickenham after her left Castle Rock following his ransacking Donna Trenton's home.

Upson, NH

The Dead Zone: Greg Stillson's scheduled Feedback Center wasn't held.

Van Drusen, PA

"Everything's Eventual": Van Drusen was near Dinky Earnshaw's hometown of Harkerville.

Vermillion Key, FL

"The Gingerbread Girl": Emily Owensby moved to her father's place on the Key for a while. She ran afoul of Jim Pickering.

Wentworth, OH

See the Locale Connections chapter.

Williams, NH

Firestarter: The Teller post office served Williams and Bradford, NH.

Woodfield, CT

"Big Driver": Tessa Jean used Royal Limousine out of Woodfield.

Appendix 2: *The Boston Post* Cane

This is based on real events. *The Boston Post* awarded canes to the oldest residents of seven hundred towns. From *Cujo* through *Needful Things*, it appeared as though Castle Rock was one of those towns:

Arnold Heebert

Cujo:

—1978: Arnold fell off the Castle Acres Nursing Home patio, broke his neck, and died. He was 101.

Aunt Evvie Chalmers

Cujo:

—1978: Aunt Evvie, 91, inherited the cane from Arnold Heebert.

—30 June 1980: Aunt Evvie died of a heart attack at her kitchen table. She was 93.

Vin Marchant

Cujo:

—1980: The cane transferred to Vin Marchant after the death of Aunt Evvie Chalmers.

Lenny Partridge

Needful Things:

—October 1991: Lenny Partridge held the cane.

In *Bag of Bones*, we learn that the cane wasn't awarded to the oldest residents of the town of Castle Rock. *The Boston Post* awarded canes in each New England county, including Castle County. They started in the 1950s.

Royce Merrill

Bag of Bones:

—19 July 1998: Royce Merrill of TR-90 died after falling down the cellar stairs. He was 95.

Ila Meserve

Bag of Bones:

—21 July 1998: TR-90's Ila Meserve received the cane at Royce Merrill's funeral service at Grace Baptist.

Clayton Brassey

Under the Dome:

—27 October 201-: Chester Mill's Clayton Brassey died.

Appendix 3: Hospitals, etc.

Many of these facilities are real. Many are not.

Acadia Mental Health Hospital

See the Organization Connections chapter.

Angels of Mercy

"1922": Hemingford City, NE

—Wilfred James when his hand became infected by a rat bite

Arapahoe County Hospital

Misery: Colorado

—Ralph Dugan, Annie Wilkes's husband, was a physical therapist.

Augusta Mental Health Institute (AMHI)

Gerald's Game: Augusta, ME

—Raymond Andrew Joubert spent a year and a half here for his unusual cruelty to animals.

Augusta State Mental Hospital

Rage: Augusta, ME

—Judge Samuel K. N. Deleavney sent Charlie Decker here until he was competent for trial.

The Dead Zone: Augusta, ME

—An early Castle Rock Strangler suspect had spent three years there.

IT: Augusta, ME

—Henry Bowers spent twenty years after taking the fall for several Derry murders.

Augusta Veterinary Clinic

The Tommyknockers: Augusta, ME

—Bobbi Anderson took her dog, Peter, to Dr. Etheridge.

Bakersfield Receiving Hospital

Misery: Bakersfield, CA

—Annie Wilkes's brother, Paul Emery Wilkes, was born here.

Bangor Mental Health Institute

IT:

—Harold Earl for drinking paint thinner

Insomnia:

—Charlie Pickering for mental issues

Bedlam Hospital

Misery: a mental institution in London

—A jealous woman had Misery Chastain committed.

Bergenfield County Hospital

The Dark Half: Bergenfield, NJ

—Dr. Hugh Pritchard removed remnants of a twin absorbed prior to birth from Thad Beaumont's brain.

Berlin Community Hospital

The Shining: Berlin, NH

—Jack Torrance's father was an orderly.

Bethesda Naval Hospital

"I Am the Doorway":

—Artie after his spaceship crashed returning from Venus

Boston Children's Hospital

"The Ten O'Clock People": Boston, MA

—Douglas Keefer was honorary chairman of their fund drive.

Boston Hospital
Boston General Hospital

The Stand: Boston, MA

—Boston General Hospital was overwhelmed with Captain Trips patients.

Needful Things

—Polly Chalmers looked forward to Boston Hospital's upcoming ultrasound therapy for her arthritis.

Boulder Hospital

Misery: Boulder, CO

—As Head Maternity Ward Nurse, Annie Wilkes killed babies with tainted formula.

Boulder City Hospital

The Stand: Boulder, CO

Boulder Community Hospital

Revival: Boulder, CO

—Les Calloway, the foreman of the music side of the business at Wolfjaw Ranch

Bowling Green Community Hospital

Lisey's Story: Bowling Green, KY

—Scott Landon after collapsing at the reception following a reading from *The Secret Pearl*

The Brandon L. Martin Psychiatric Center

Revival: Kailua, HI

—Conrad Morton, semi-catatonic, after trying to kill his partner then himself

Briar Ridge

The Green Mile:

—Percy Wetmore was sent to the state-run hospital when he become catatonic.

Bridgton Hospital

Doctor Sleep: Maine

—They found nothing wrong when Abra Stone wouldn't stop crying the morning of 9/11/2001.

Brigham and Women's Hospital

Blaze: Boston, MA

—Blaze worked in the laundry for about three years.

Doctor Sleep: Boston, MA

—Abra Stone was born here.

Castle County General Hospital
Castle Rock Hospital

Bag of Bones:

—Royce Merrill after falling down the cellar stairs. He died in a coma the next day.

Gwendy's Magic Feather:

—Mrs. Peterson after it appeared her cancer may have returned

Note: By the mid-1990s, Castle Rock got their own hospital. Prior to *Bag of Bones*, Central Maine General and Northern Cumberland Hospital served Castle Rock.

Castle Rock Meadows Nursing Home

Gwendy's Final Task: Castle Rock, ME

—Mr. Peterson

Castle View Nursing Home

Gwendy's Final Task: Castle Rock, ME

—Mr. Peterson

Catherine Russell Hospital, aka Cathy Russell

Under the Dome: Chester's Mill, ME

—Big Jim Rennie for heart arrhythmia; Junior Rennie for a brain tumor

Central Hospital

Roadwork: M_____, W_____

—a client of The Blue Ribbon Laundry

Central Maine General Hospital (CMG)
Central Maine Medical Center (CMMC)

'Salem's Lot:

—Danny Glick for delayed emotional shock after Ralphie disappeared

—Tony Glick for shock after his wife died

Rage: Mr. Carlson was treated at CMG when Charlie Decker hit him with a wrench.

"The Woman in the Room": Lewiston, ME

—Johnny's mother after a botched cordotomy operation

"The Body":

—Chris Chambers several times after beatings from his father

"Gramma": Lewiston, ME

—Buddy Bruckner from breaking a leg at home plate

Lisey's Story: Auburn, ME

—Darla Debusher got six stitches over her left eye in the ER after a fight with Amanda Debusher over Richie Stanchfield.

"Riding the Bullet": CMMC in Lewiston, ME

—Jean Parker after a stroke

The Dark Tower: Lewiston, ME

—Stephen King after Bryan Smith struck him with his minivan

Under the Dome: Lewiston, ME

—Ollie Dinsmore after being rescued from under the Dome

11/22/63: Lewiston, ME

—Bill Laidlaw (Al Templeton) for a feigned heart attack

Doctor Sleep:

—A CT scan confirmed Billy Freeman's aortic aneurysm.

"Mr. Harrigan's Phone":

—A transfer student from Vermont was hospitalized after a hazing incident at Gates Falls Middle.

Central New Hampshire (CNH) Hospital

Doctor Sleep: New Hampshire

—served the town of Frazier

Central State Psychiatric

"Ur": Kentucky

City of Angels Hospital

Later: New York City

—Kenneth Alan Therriault was an orderly.

City General

Rose Madder:

—Rose Daniels after a miscarriage following a Norman Daniels beating

"The Life of Chuck":

—Felicia Anderson was a nurse.

City Receiving Hospital

"The Mangler":

—Annette Gillian after being severely burned from the mangler's broken steam lines

Cleaves Mills Community Hospital

The Dead Zone: Cleaves Mills, ME

the Cleveland Clinic

11/22/63:

—George Amberson thought Mimi Simmons should seek cancer treatment at the Clinic instead of Mexico.

Elevation:

—Scott Carey didn't want to be their guinea pig because of his weight loss.

Congress Memorial Hospital

"Morality":

—They laid off Nora Callahan.

County General

The Regulators:

—Hugh Hobart after breaking his hip and leg in a fall down the stairs

County Hospital

Dolores Claiborne:

—Joe St. George for an autopsy

County Hospital

The Green Mile:

—John Coffey after his execution

County Memorial

The Colorado Kid: Tinnock, ME

Crestview Nursing Home

Sleeping Beauties: Dooling, WV

—Roger Dunphy looted jewelry from women with the Aurora Sleeping Sickness.

Cumberland General

The Dead Zone: Cumberland, ME

—Vera Smith, Johnny's mother, after having a stroke watching Johnny's uncomfortable news conference

Cumberland Memorial Hospital

"It Grows on You":

—Dana Roy died of intestinal cancer.

Cumberland Receiving Hospital

'Salem's Lot: Cumberland, ME

—Matt Burke for a heart attack when the Undead Mike Ryerson visited

—Ben Mears after Floyd Tibbits beat him up

the Dakota Ridge Medical Center

The Stand: Boulder, CO

—Dr. George Richardson set up shop here.

Dean McGee Eye Institute

The Outsider: Oklahoma City, OK

—Shards of lens injured a TV cameraman when Ralph Anderson's stray shot hit his camera.

Denver Receiving Hospital

Misery: Denver, CO

—Annie Wilkes killed a patient.

Derry Hospital
Derry Home Hospital
Home Hospital

"Mrs. Todd's Shortcut": Derry, ME

IT: Derry, ME

—Dorsey Corcoran died here after his stepfather fractured his skull with a hammer.

—Audra Denbrough spent time here after being taken by IT.

—They sedated Sharon Denbrough after Georgie's death.

—Mike Hanlon and cabbie Dave were born in this hospital. Mike went back after Henry Bowers stabbed his leg about thirty-eight years later.

—They fixed Eddie Kaspbrak's broken arm.

—Al Marsh, Beverly's father, was a hospital janitor.

The Tommyknockers:

—Hilly Brown after the shock of losing his brother in Altair-4

Insomnia:

—Faye Chapin, a Harris Avenue Old Crock, after a heart attack

—Helen Deepneau after Ed Deepneau beat her up for signing a petition to have Susan Day speak on behalf of WomanCare in Derry

—Bob Polhurst, dying of pneumonia, after he stopped breathing temporarily

—Carolyn Roberts for a brain tumor, which took her away from Ralph

—Jimmy V. for cancer

Bag of Bones:

—Mrs. Deorsey was treated and released after the car accident Joanna Noonan witnessed

Lisey's Story:

—Lisey Debusher wanted to take Scott Landon to the ER when he offered her a blood-bool. He declined.

"Fair Extension":

—An MRI showed Dave Streeter's tumors had shrunk. Four months later, Norma Goodhugh's MRI showed breast cancer had spread to her lymph nodes.

Doctors Hospital

Misert: Queens, New York, NY

—Paul Sheldon was admitted after escaping Annie Wilkes.

Doctors Hospital

Roadwork: M_____, W_____

—Charlie Dawes, Bart and Mary's son, was diagnosed with a brain tumor here.

Eastern [Maine] General Hospital
Eastern Maine Medical Center (EMMC)

The Dead Zone: Bangor, ME

—Johnny Smith after his accident with the drag-racing Brad Freneau

—Mary Thibault, Brad's girlfriend, after the same accident; she didn't make it

—Dennis Hazlett, Sarah and Walt's son, was born here.

Cujo

Pet Sematary:

—Norma Crandall's friend Betty Coslaw died of cancer here.

—Norma Crandall after a minor heart attack. Doctor Louis Creed's presence may have saved her life.

—Hannibal Benson started the Eastern General Hospital fund before World War II.

IT: Bangor, ME

The Tommyknockers

The Dark Half:

—Thad Beaumont had a CAT-scan and cranial X-rays.

East Side Receiving Hospital

Rose Madder:

—Cynthia Smith after Norm Daniels beat her.

Ebert Animal Hospital

"If It Bleeds": Youngstown, OH

—Lucky, a golden retriever, after being gutted and left for dead in a ditch. Lucky didn't make it.

Edith Nourse Rogers veterans' hospital

Under the Dome: Massachusetts

—Conscientious-objector Thurston Marshall was an orderly for two years during the Vietnam War.

Eliot

Doctor Sleep:

—Normie Lloyd would die of Gaucher's disease before he turned ten.

Eliot Nursing Home

"Rita Hayworth and Shawshank Redemption":

—Shawshank State Prison did their laundry.

the Emily Cathcart Clinic

Cell: Waltham, MA

—an abortion clinic that people protested against

Estes Park Community Hospital

The Shining's "After the Play":

—Wendy Torrance after being beaten by the Overlook Hotel-possessed Jack Torrance

Flint City General Hospital

The Outsider: Flint City, OK

—Fred Peterson after a failed hanging attempt

—Detective Betsy Riggins to have a baby

the Ford City Veterinary Clinic

"Ayana": Ford City, PA

—Doc Gentry consulted at the clinic

French County Lutheran Hospital

Black House: Arden, WI

—Judy Marshall recovered in the mental ward after the Fisherman took her son, Tyler, for the Crimson King.

Gage Point

Gerald's Game: Hancock County

—Raymond Andrew Joubert was in this detox/halfway house/mental institution until he was nineteen for gross sexual abuse.

the Good Life Retirement Home

"Cookie Jar":

—Rhett Alderson

Grace of Mary Hospital

Doctor Sleep: Wilmington, NC

—Dan Torrance was an orderly.

Greenlawn Recovery and Rehabilitation

Lisey's Story: the Twin Cities in Maine (Lewiston-Auburn)

—Amanda Debusher after hurting herself in a Big Tantrum and sliding into a catatonic state

Groves of Healing Hospital

"Ayana": Connecticut

—Gentry sneaked into a dying three-year-old boy's room and healed him.

Harriet White Memorial Hospital

"The Breathing Method": New York, NY

—The pregnant Sandra Stanchfield died after an empty ambulance departing the hospital crashed into her cab. Dr. Emlyn McCarron saved her baby boy before she expired.

Hartford Receiving Hospital

"The Boogeyman": Hartford, CT

—Shirl Billings for an autopsy after the boogeyman killed her

Harvest Hills Special Care Unit

"Batman and Robin Have an Altercation": San Antonio, TX

—Dougie Sanderson's father had Alzheimer's.

Heaven's Bay Community Hospital

Joyland: Heaven's Bay, NC

—Eddie Parks after a heart attack

Helen Rivington House

Doctor Sleep: a hospice in Frazier, NH

—As Doctor Sleep, Dan Torrance helped people when they died.

Hemingford County Hospital

"Afterlife": Hemingford County, NE

—Bill Andrews was born in this hospital.

the Henry Glassman Clinic

Thinner: New Jersey

—Billy Halleck underwent a three-day series of metabolic tests to explain his weight loss. Three doctors each presented a different diagnosis.

Hernandez General Hospital

Misery:

—Annie Wilkes had caused her father to trip over a pile of clothes and fall down the stairs. He died at the hospital.

Indianola General Hospital

The Green Mile: Indianola

—Melinda Moores to get tests for a brain tumor

—Wild Bill Wharton for tests after faking seizures in court

Juniper Hill

See the Organization Connections chapter.

Kennebec Valley Hospital

Needful Things

—Nettie Cobb and Wilma Jerzyck were taken to the morgue for autopsies.

Kindred Hospital

The Outsider: Dayton, OH

—Alzheimer's patient Peter Maitland lived in their Heisman Memory Unit.

John M. Kiner Memorial Hospital
Ralph M. Kiner Memorial Hospital

Mr. Mercedes: John M. Kiner Memorial

—many people Mr. Mercedes ran over in the City Center Massacre

—Bill Hodges after a heart attack

Finders Keepers: John M. Kiner Memorial Hospital

—Linda Saubers after Morris Bellamy's bullet grooved the right side of her head

End of Watch: Ralph M. Kiner Memorial Hospital

—Martin Stover after the Mercedes Killer ran over her

—Barbara Robinson after getting hit by a truck in Lowtown

—Bill Hodges for pancreatic cancer treatment

"If It Bleeds": John M. Kiner Memorial Hospital

—Barb and Jerome Robinson after being "mugged" by Chet Ondowsky

Kingdom [Hospital]

Lisey's Story: Auburn, ME

Kittery Receiving Hospital

"Rita Hayworth and Shawshank Redemption"

—Shawshank State Prison did their laundry.

L.A. General

"Umney's Last Case"

—A Cuban bandleader died here.

La Riviere General

Black House: La Riviere, WI

—Charles Burnside showed up one day. They sent him to Maxton Elder Care.

—Little Nancy Hale died there after getting too close to Black House.

the Lakes Region Traumatic Brain Injury Clinic (TBI)

Mr. Mercedes: part of John M. Kiner Memorial

—Brady Hartsfield lay in a coma with limited brain function after Holly Gibney walloped him on the head with the Happy Slapper.

Finders Keepers: part of John M. Kiner Memorial Hospital

—Brady Hartsfield had woken from his coma but was semi-catatonic.

Lakeview Assisted Living Center

"Mister Yummy": Nebraska

—Dave Calhoun, Ollie Franklin, and Olga Glukhov

Lenox Hill Hospital

Later:

—Jamie Conklin was born in Lenox Hill.

Lewiston General Hospital

The Dead Zone: Lewiston, ME

—Chuck Spier after losing an eye when the battery exploded while jump starting his truck

Libertyville Community Hospital

Christine: Libertyville, PA

—Dennis Guilder after a football injury

the Loving Hands Hospice

Sleeping Beauties: Georgetown, DC

—early Aurora cases on the East Coast

Maine Medical
Maine Medical Center

Blaze:

—Norma Gerard after Blaze cold-cocked her while kidnapping Joseph Gerard IV

"Rat":

—Al Stamper for routine cancer tests

Massachusetts General (Mass General) Hospital

Dreamcatcher:

—Jonesy after being clobbered by a car when he crossed the street, thinking he saw Duddits after many years

The Dark Tower:

—Hospital oncologists told Coretta Vele her brain tumor was malignant.

11/22/63:

—Dr. Ellerton added Mark Anderson from Mass General to the team of plastic surgeons for Sadie Dunhill's facial reconstruction.

Doctor Sleep:

—Nurse Sarah Olson moved from Helen Rivington House to Mass General.

—Chetta Reynolds after shattering an arm

Elevation:

—Scott Carey had no interest in having Mass General study his weight loss.

Massachusetts Memorial Hosptial

"The Sun Dog":

—a Mad Hatter after her cat tore into her ear at a séance

the Mayo Clinic

Roadwork:

—Salvatore Magliore had a cataract removed.

Thinner: Minnesota

—Judge Cary Rossington checked in after Taduz Lemke cursed him with reptile-like scales.

Needful Things:

—Their unaffordable ultrasound therapy might have been able to help Polly Chalmers's arthritis.

Elevation:

—Scott Carey wasn't about to check into the Mayo Clinic to have his odd weight loss studied.

Billy Summers:

McDowell Hospital

Sleeping Beauties: McDowell County, WV

MedNow

Later: an urgent-care facility in Redfield, NY

—Officer Caroline took Jamie Conklin to get checked out after Liz Dutton had kidnapped him.

MedStar Hospital

The Institute: Washington, DC

—US Representative Mark Berkowitz died following a car crash the Institute caused.

Mercy Hospital

"If It Bleeds": Pineborough Township, PA

—many victims of Chet Ondowsky's bomb at Albert Macready Middle School

Mercy General Hospital

The Stand: Brooklyn, NY

—Alice Underwood, Larry's mother, with Captain Trips

"Thin Scenery":

—Harold Crosby had a fake MRI test at Mercy General.

Mercy Hospital

Misery: Los Angeles, CA

—Annie Wilkes's roommate, Andrea Saint James, died after tripping over a dead cat at the top of the stairs.

Mercy Hospital

The Outsider: Flint City, OK

—Arlene Peterson after a heart attack

Mercy Hospital

Gwendy's Magic Feather: Portland, ME

—Johnathon Riordan with AIDS

Merrimack Valley Hosptial

Doctor Sleep:

—Frederika Bimmel had stomach cancer.

Metropolitan Hospital

"Stationary Bike":

—Richard Sifkitz's physical examination showed high cholesterol.

Mosconi's Veterinary Clinic

"The Jaunt": New Paltz, NY

—Mosconi dissected Victor Carune's first mouse Jaunt-test subject.

Motton Receiving Hospital

Carrie: Motton, ME

—three injured firemen on Prom Night

the Murfreesboro, GA, General Hospital

The Stand: Murfreesboro, GA

—Sam Tauber's mother. (While picking blackberries, Sam fell in a well, broke both legs, and died the next morning.)

Nashville Memorial Hospital

Lisey's Story: Nashville, TN

—Scott Landon after Gerd Allen Cole shot him

New York General

The Dark Tower: New York, NY

—Lupe Delgado with AIDS from a Type Three vampire

Newark General

"Blockade Billy": Newark, NJ

Northern Cumberland Hospital
Northern Cumberland Memorial Hospital

Cujo: Bridgton, ME

—Donna Trenton after her ordeal with Cujo in Camber's dooryard

Needful Things: Bridgton, ME

—Newton Chalmers, Polly's father

—Scott Garson with extensive injuries after Buster Keeton ran him down in a Cadillac

—Lenny Priest after Hugh Priest beat him up pretty good

—Norris Ridgewick after Ace Merrill shot him

—Brian Rusk after guilt in his part in the deaths of Nettie Cobb and Wilma Jerzyck made him sick

—Sean Ruck for shock after his brother died

Gerald's Game:

—A Rescue Services ambulance took Jessie Burlingame to this hospital after she escaped the handcuffs.

The Dark Tower: Bridgton, ME

—Character Stephen King was pronounced dead after being struck by a van while walking on Route 7.

Nashville Memorial Hospital

Lisey's Story: Nashville, TN

—Scott Landon after Gerd Allen Cole shot him

Oak Cove Asylum

The Plant: Cutlersville, NY

—General Heckler stabbed three people in his escape.

Our Sisters of Charity Hospital

Pet Sematary: Chicago, IL

Oxford Hills Hospital

Gerald's Game

Parkland Hospital

The Talisman:

—After sending Ferd Janklow to the Pit for an escape attempt, Sunlight Gardener fibbed that Ferd was recovering in Parkland Hospital.

Parkland Memorial Hospital

11/22/63: Dallas, TX

—Sadie Dunhill after Johnny Clayton cut her (in two timelines)

—George Amberson after Akiva Roth had him beaten

Portland City Hospital

Gerald's Game:

—Jessie Mahout was a candy-striper.

Blaze:

—John Cheltzman died after rheumatic fever had been misdiagnosed as the flu.

Portland General Hospital

See the Organization Connections chapter.

Portsmouth General Hospital

Joyland: Portsmouth, NH

—Timothy Jones after a heart attack

Presbyterian

"Red Screen":

—Lennie Crocker died from blood loss.

the Pussy Palace, a V.A. hospital

Hearts in Atlantis: San Francisco, CA

—John Sullivan and Willie Shearman after a helicopter crash near the Dong Ha Province

Quigly, OH, Veteran's Hospital

"The Old Dude's Ticker:

—Robert S. Deisonhoff was sent home from Vietnam to be treated for combat fatigue.

Riverside Hospital

The Dark Tower: New York City

—Rowan Magruder had room 577; Rowan died, then Don Callahan got the room.

Riverview Hospital

Misery: Harrisburg, PA

—Annie Wilkes killed a couple of patients.

Rockland Memorial

Billy Summers: Red Bluff, AR

—Wanda Stubbs for a head wound after being robbed at Zoney's Go Mart

Rolling Hills Elder Care Center

"If It Bleeds": near Cleveland, OH

—Holly Gibney's Uncle Henry

Saint Joseph's Hospital

Misery: New Hampshire

—Annie Wilkes killed several terminally ill patients.

the Sanford Hospital

The Stand: Sanford, ME

—Carla Goldsmith, Frannie's mother, with Captain Trips

—Will Ronson from the drugstore with Captain Trips

Santo Donato General Hospital

"Apt Pupil": Santo Donato, CA

—Arthur Denker after a heart attack he suffered while digging a grave for one of his victims

—Morris Heisel after falling from a ladder while repairing his rain gutters. He recognized Denker as a Nazi war criminal.

Sarasota Memorial Hospital

Duma Key: Sarasota, FL

—Edgar Freemantle took Wireman when Wireman lost the sight in his left eye.

—Elizabeth Eastlake died after a seizure.

"A Very Tight Place": Sarasota, FL

—They treated Tim Grunwald for lung cancer.

Later: Sarasota, FL

—Professor Burkett's friend Dave Robertson was unconscious following a stroke.

Serenity Hill

See the Organization Connections chapter.

Sisters of Mary Hospital

The Dark Tower: 23rd Street in New York

—Odetta Holmes / Detta Walker after Jack Mort pushed her in front of the A-train subway

Squirrel Hill Receiving

The Cannibals (unpublished): River City

—Pamela Andeyric spent a couple of days in the hospital after having two impacted wisdom teeth extracted.

St. Anne's Hospital

"The Moving Finger":

—CPA Howard Mitla's new tax account with them was a rat's nest.

St. Francis

Revival: Tulsa, OK

St. Francis Hospital and Medical Center

The Dark Tower: Topeka, KS, in a world similar to ours

—Dr. Morris Hackford estimated the superflu death toll.

St. Joe's

A Face in the Crowd: near Shrewsbury, MA

—Lester Embree's mother worked in the laundry.

St. Joseph's

Blaze: Providence, RI

—George Rackley was born in the charity ward of this Catholic hospital.

St. Jude's

"Ayana": Connecticut

—Gentry healed a woman dying in the hospital.

St. Luke's

End of Watch: Phoenix, AZ

—a woman after falling into a stack of rebar on a Habitat for Humanity project

St. Mary's

Rose Madder:

—Rose Daniels spent three days after a Norman Daniels beating. A broken rib had almost punctured a lung.

St. Mary's Hospital

Roadwork: M_____, W_____

—Johnny Walker died there after a Pontiac slid through a red light and hit his Blue Ribbon Laundry van.

St. Stephen's

"A Good Marriage":

—A biopsy found an infected lymph node in Robert Anderson's left armpit.

St. Stephens Hospital (St. Stevie's)

Revival: Castle Rock, ME

"Premium Harmony": Castle Rock, ME

—Mary Burkett after a fatal heart attack

St. Theresa's (St. Terry's)

Sleeping Beauties: Dooling County, WV

—Yvette Quinn's twin baby girls and Tiffany Jones were the first patients with a strange sleeping sickness.

Stephens Memorial Hospital

Lisey's Story: Norway-South Paris, ME

—Amanda Debusher after cutting herself

Under the Dome: Norway-South Paris, ME

Stormont-Vail Regional Medical Center

The Dark Tower: in a world similar to ours

—Dr. April Montoya estimated six to twelve people were sick for each person the superflu had killed.

Sunny Acres

Mr. Mercedes: Warsaw County

—Edith Wharton spent a few weeks in this nursing home.

Togus, a VA mental hospital

"The Body":

—Norman Duchamp, Teddy's father, was sent here after he burned Teddy's ears on a hot stove burner.

Needful Things:

—Ronnie Keeton, Danforth's father, spent four years in the mental wing.

Topeka State Hospital

The Dark Tower: Topeka, KS, in a world similar to ours

Utica Soldiers' Hospital

The Tommyknockers: Utica, NY

—Bobbi Anderson's father died here.

Walter Reed

The Outsider:

—Heath Holmes worked at Walter Reed for five years.

Warsaw County Memorial Hospital

Mr. Mercedes: Warsaw County

—Edith Wharton died here after a stroke.

Weston State

Sleeping Beauties: This West Virginia asylum closed in 1994.

Westover Doctors Hospital

Carrie: Westover, ME

—Margaret White for a miscarriage

Westover Mercy Hospital

Carrie: Westover, ME

—Carrie for an autopsy

Appendix 4: Funeral Homes

Abbot-Wexler Funeral Parlor

Duma Key: Sarasota, FL

—Miss Elizabeth Eastlake

Bowie Funeral Home

Under the Dome: Chester's Mill, ME

—Lester Coggins

—Arletta Coombs

—Shelley Dinsmore

—Gertrude Evans

—Lois and Will Freeman

—Angie McCain

—Chief Perkins; Brenda Perkins

—Claudette Sanders; Dodee Sanders

—Chuck Thompson

Broadview & Sons

Gwendy's Final Task: St. Louis, MO

—Lawrence Winston III

Brookings-Smith Mortuary

Pet Sematary: Bangor, ME

—Norma Crandall

—Gage Creed

Insomnia:

—Carolyn Roberts

Castings Brothers

"1922": Hemingford Home, NE

—Henry James

Crosman's

Under the Dome: Castle Rock, ME

—Many Chester's Mill residents preferred them.

Crowder's Funeral Home

Sleeping Beauties: Dooling, WV

Curtis Funeral Home, aka Curtis Mortuary

The Stand: Shoyo, AR

—Jane Baker's and John Baker's families always used Curtis Mortuary.

Dakin's Funeral Home

Bag of Bones: Motton, ME

—Lance Devore (Mattie's husband)

—Jo Noonan

Despegni Funeral Parlor

Bag of Bones: Bridgeport, CT

—across from The Corner Pocket

Donelli Brothers Funeral Home

The Outsider: Flint City, OK

—Frankie Peterson, Arelene Peterson, Ollie Peterson

the Ebert-Holloway Funeral Parlor

"The Life of Chuck":

—Albie Krantz, Chuck's grandfather

Foreman Funeral Home, aka Foreman's Mortuary

'Salem's Lot: Jerusalem's Lot, ME

—Danny Glick

—Mike Ryerson

Foster's Funeral Home

Misery: New Hampshire

—Hester "Queenie" Beaulifant, an Annie Wilkes victim

Geordie & Sons

Doctor Sleep: Frazier, NH

—Mrs. Eleanor Ouellette

Green's Mortuary

'Salem's Lot: Cumberland, ME

—Mrs. Glick

Greenspan Funeral Home

Pet Sematary: Ludlow, ME

—Timmy Baterman

Hay & Peabody's Funeral Home

Needful Things: Castle Rock, ME

—Lorraine Chalmers, Polly's mother

"It Grows on You":

—Joe Newall

"Mr. Harrigan's Phone":

—Mr. John Harrigan

Heartfield & Son Funeral Home

Black House: French Landing, WI

—near the library and police station

Jaquard's Funeral Home

Bag of Bones: Motton, ME

—They handled shipping Max Devore's body to Palm Springs, CA.

Hines Funeral Parlor & Mortuary

"A Death: Dakota Territory

—Jim Trusdale after he was hanged for the murder of little Rebecca Cline

Mercier Funeral Home

Dolores Claiborne: Little Tall Island, ME

—Joe St. George

Peabody's Funeral Home

Revival: Gates Falls, ME

—Patsy Jacobs and Morrie Jacobs

Plainville Funeral Home

The Outsider: Plainville, TX

—The Plainville Funeral Home transported the bodies of Howie Gold, Jack Hoskins, and Alec Pelley from Texas to Flint City, OK.

Shady Rest Mortuary

The Plant: Long Island

—General Heckslerfaked his death in the crematorium furnace.

Soames Funeral Home

Mr. Mercedes:

—Mrs. Olivia Trelawney

—Mrs. Elizabeth Wharton (Mrs. Trelawney's mother)

Soames's Mortuary

11/22/63: Jodie, TX

Tinnock Funeral Home

The Colorado Kid: Tinnock, ME

—James Cogan, aka the Colorado Kid and known only as John Doe at the time, after choking to death on Hammock Beach

Yarbrough Funeral Home

"The Life of Chuck"

Appendix 5: Cemeteries

Arlington National Cemetery

11/22/63:

—Sadie Dunhill

The Birches

The Dead Zone: Pownal, ME

—A family of Marstens is buried at The Birches. We don't know whether they are related to Hubie.

—Generations of Bowdens have been laid to rest at The Birches, but we don't know whether they are related to the Bowden family of "Apt Pupil." Todd Bowden and his family lived in Santo Donato, CA, and no family history is given.

—Pillsburys have been buried there since 1750.

—John Smith

"Gramma": on the Maple Sugar Road

Castle View Cemetery

"The Body": Castle Rock, ME

—Dennis Lachance, Gordie's older brother, who was killed in a Jeep accident at Fort Benning, GA

Chilton Remembrance Cemetery

Gerald's Game:

—Raymond Andrew Joubert removed the noses from two corpses.

the Cowboy Graveyard

The Outsider: Canning Township, OK

—abandoned

—Terry Maitland's ancestors

Crestwood Cemetery

"In a Half-World of Terror": Belwood District, California

—Danny Gerard and Rankin stole Daniel Wheatherby's body for Steffen Weinbaum.

Dartmouth Crossing Cemetery

Firestarter: Hastings Glen, NY, three miles from the Manders farm

Dunwich Cemetery

"The Sun Dog": Dunwich, MA

Elm Cemetery

"Mr. Harrigan's Phone: Harlow, ME

—Mr. John Harrigan

Fairlawn Cemetery

Bag of Bones: Derry, ME

—Joanna Noonan after dying from a brain aneurysm

Fairlawn

End of Watch:

—Bill Hodges died of pancreatic cancer.

Grace Cemetery

The Dark Half: Castle Rock, ME

Groveland

Pet Sematary: Chicago, IL

—Louis Creed's Uncle Carl oversaw an exhumation from a grave with a sealing vault.

Harmony Hill Cemetery

'Salem's Lot: one of three in Jerusalem's Lot, ME

—Danny Glick was almost buried in Harmony Hill Cemetery.

—Hubert Marsten, "God Grant He Lie Still"

Hillview

The Outsider: Flint City, OH

—almost full

Homeland Cemetery

The Tommyknockers: Haven, ME

—Ruth McCausland

APPENDIX 5

The Dark Half: Castle Rock, ME

—Danforth Keeton's father and uncle

—George Stark, for about a week

"The Sun Dog": Castle Rock, ME

—Pop Merrill's mother

Needful Things:

—Polly Chalmers's great-aunt Evelyn

—Nettie Cobb and Wilma Jerzyck after killing one another

—Homer Gamache's body was found nearby.

—Bill Keeton, Danforth's uncle

Gwendy's Magic Feather: Castle Rock, ME

—Sheriff George Bannerman

—Olive Kepnes

—Pop Merrill

Gwendy's Final Task: Castle Rock, ME

—Alicia Peterson

Gerald's Game:

—Sheriff Ridgewick and Deputy LaPointe caught Raymond Andrew Joubert on his way to Homeland Cemetery for collectible body parts.

"It Grows On You":

—Joe Newall's baby girl was laid to rest in a Gates Falls cemetery instead of Homeland.

—Gary Paulson was buried here. Joe Newall's house grew a new cupola.

Libertyville Heights Cemetery

Christine: Libertyville, PA

—the Cunninghams: Arnie, Michael, and Regina

—Rita LeBay then years later, Roland LeBay

Longview Cemetery

11/22/63: Derry, ME

—Frank Dunning's parents

Mary Cyr Cemetery

Misery: New Hampshire

—Hester "Queenie" Beaulifant, a victim of Annie Wilkes

Memorial Park Cemetery

The Outsider: Flint City, OH

—Terry Maitland

Milford Cemetery

"Sometimes They Come Back": Milford, CT

—Vincent Corey, David Garcia, and Robert Lawson. They came back.

Mission Hill

"Batman and Robin Have an Altercation": San Antonio, TX

—Reggie Sanderson after a 16-year-old drunk driver killed him

Mount Hope Cemetery

The Stand: Peoria, IL, near Judge Farris

Pet Sematary: Bangor, ME

—Norma Crandall, in plot H-101 after the spring thaw

IT: Derry, ME

—Georgie Denbrough

"1408":

—Mike Enslin wrote about the cemetery's Barking Ghost.

Noggin Mound Cemetery

Black House: in or near French Landing, WI

—Rhoda Gilbertson Leyden after liver cancer took her

The Oaks

Dolores Claiborne: Little Tall Island, ME

—Joe St. George

Peace Cemetery

"A Good Marriage": Yarmouth, ME

—Bob Anderson (serial killer Beadie) after his wife killed him.

Peaceful Rest Cemetery

The Outsider: Regis, OH

—Heath Holmes, Mavis Holmes (Heath's mother), and Heath's father

the Pet Sematary

Pet Sematary: Ludlow, ME

—Biffer, "A HELLUVA SNIFFER"

—Bowser, Billy Holloway's mongrel

—Mrs. Bradleigh's parakeet, the second time it died

—one of Old Man Fritchie's racing pigeons that a dog killed

—three of Albion Groatley's barn cats

—Hannah, "THE BEST DOG THAT EVER LIVED"

—Pete LaVasseur's dog

—Marta, a rabbit

—Gen. Patton, a "GOOD! DOG!"

—Polynesia (Polly), a parrot

—Ringo, a hamster

—Matty Ryder's raccoon

—Smucky the Cat, "HE WAS OBEDIANT"

—Jud Crandall's dog, Spot, the second time he died

—Trixie, a pet "KILT ON THE HIGHEWAY"

Placerville Cemetery

Rage: Placerville, ME

—Dicky Cable, who had beaten up Charlie Decker at Carol Granger's birthday party

Pleasant Hill Cemetery

"The Mangler": five miles from the Blue Ribbon Laundry

Pleasant Ridge Cemetery

Under the Dome: Chester's Mill, ME

—Francine Rennie

Pleasantview Cemetery

Pet Sematary: Bangor, ME

—Timmy Baterman; he didn't stay

—Gage Creed; he didn't stay, either

—Phipps, near Gage Creed's plot; as far as we know, Phipps stayed

Sabbatus Vale Cemetery

Lisey's Story: Sabbatus Falls, ME

—Good Ma and Dandy Debusher, Lisey's parents; Grampy and Granny D, too

Schoolyard Hill Cemetery

'Salem's Lot: another of three cemeteries in Jerusalem's Lot, ME

—Shakers, an extinct New England colony

Seaview Cemetery

The Colorado Kid:

—James Cogan, aka the Colorado Kid and known only as John Doe at the time, after choking to death on Hammock Beach

Serenity Ridge Cemetery

"N.": up on Boy Hill in Motton, ME

Shady Hills Cemetery

Sleeping Beauties: Dooling, WV

—Archie Coates

St. Cyril's church graveyard

11/22/63: Lisbon Falls, ME

—George T. Amberson

Stackpole Cemetery

The Dark Half: Castle Rock, ME

Stokes's burying parlor

The Dark Tower: Tree Village, Mid-World

—Big Ross after being killed in the Endless Forest

Wayvern Hill

"The Library Policeman": Junction City, IA

West Hill Cemetery

11/22/63: Jodie, TX

—Vince Knowles

West Side Cemetery

Hearts in Atlantis: Harwich, CT

—Sully-John

Cell: Rochester, NH

—Armed normies protected a flock of phone-crazies roosting in the cemetery.

Willow Grove Cemetery

Revival: Harlow, ME

—Patsy Jacobs and Morrie Jacobs

Woodlawn Cemetery

Later: the Bronx

—Liz Dutton drove Jamie Conklin through the cemetery to see whether he saw any dead people.

Appendix 6: *Desperation / The Regulators* Character Comparison

Stephen King and Richard Bachman eerily used many of the same character names in their respective novels released on the same day, but they were different characters. They were not the same characters appearing in different books, is what I mean to say.

Steve Ames

Desperation:

—Steven Andrew Ames
—from Lubbock, TX
—drove a Ryder Truck

The Regulators:

—Steven Jay Ames
—grew up in Texas
—drove a Ryder Truck

Tom Billingsley

Desperation:

—a Desperation, NV, resident
—a retired veterinarian

The Regulators:

—a Wentworth, OH, resident
—a retired veterinarian

David Carver

Desperation: a child

—lived
—a Wentworth, OH, resident

The Regulators: an adult
—died in Wentworth, OH
—a Wentworth resident

Ellen Carver

Desperation: an adult
—died in Desperation, NV
—a Wentworth, OH, resident

The Regulators: a child
—lived
—a Wentworth, OH, resident

Kirsten (Pie) Carver

Desperation: an adult
—died in Desperation, NV
—a Wentworth, OH, resident

The Regulators: a child
—died in Wentworth, OH
—a Wentworth resident

Ralph Carver

Desperation: an adult
—died in Desperation, NV
—a Wentworth, OH, resident

The Regulators: a child
—lived
—a Wentworth, OH, resident

Collie Entragian

Desperation:

—died in Desperation, NV
—a crazy cop
—a Desperation resident

The Regulators:

—died in Wentworth, OH
—an ex-cop
—a Wentworth resident

Frank Geller

Desperation:

—died in Desperation, NV
—the Desperation Mining Corporation chief mining engineer

The Regulators:

—lived
—a Wentworth, OH, resident

Bill Harris

Desperation:

—Johnny Marinville's literary agent

The Regulators:

—Johnny Marinville's literary agent

Mary Jackson

Desperation:

—lived
—had a miscarriage

—showed mid-life crisis by lashing out at being called "ma'am"

The Regulators:

—died in Wentworth, OH

—had a miscarriage

—showed mid-life crisis by sleeping with another man

Brad Josephson

Desperation:

—died in Desperation, NV

—the Desperation Mining Corp. receptionist

The Regulators:

—died in Wentworth, OH

—a Wentworth resident

Little Bitty Baby Smitty

Desperation:

—a character in a naughty rhyme

The Regulators:

—a character in a naughty rhyme

Lushan

Desperation:

—the Lushan brothers

—worked in the mine

The Regulators:

—Lushan Chinese Laundry in *The Regulators* movie

Johnny Marinville

Desperation:

—died in Desperation, NV
—a New York resident
—a National Book Award novelist
—first ex-wife: Terry; inspired a new book
—had a Harley
—56

The Regulators:

—lived
—a Wentworth, OH, resident
—a children's book writer and National Book Award novelist
—first ex-wife: Terry; inspired a new book
—had a Harley
—in his 60s

Gene Martin

Desperation:

—a Reverend

The Regulators:

—an accountant

Flip Moran

Desperation:

—a Desperation townsperson

The Regulators:

—a character in a movie

MotoKops

Desperation:
—cartoon characters

The Regulators:
—cartoon characters that came to life and wreaked havoc in Wentworth, OH

Joe Prudum

Desperation:
—a Desperation Mining Corporation night watchman

The Regulators:
—a character in a movie

Billy Rancourt

Desperation:
—a Desperation townsperson

The Regulators:
—a character in a movie

Jim Reed

Desperation: an adult
—died in Desperation, NV
—Desperation, NV's Town Safety Officer

The Regulators: a child
—died in Wentworth, OH
—a Wentworth resident

Cary Ripton

Desperation: an adult
—died in Desperation, NV
—a Desperation Mining Corporation pit-foreman

The Regulators: a child
—died in Wentworth, OH
—a Wentworth paperboy

Debbie Ross

Desperation: an adult
—lived (stayed in Wentworth, OH)
—a Wentworth resident

The Regulators: a child
—died in Wentworth, OH
—a Wentworth resident

Sally

Desperation:
—a horse

The Regulators:
—a Deep Earth Mining Corporation employee

Mr. Smiley-Smile

Desperation:
—Deirdre Finney coined the term

The Regulators:
—author Richard Bachman used the term

Cynthia Smith

Desperation:

—lived

—returning home after leaving a few years before

The Regulators:

—lived

—a clerk at E-Z Stop 24 in Wentworth, OH

Gary Soderson

Desperation:

—lived

The Regulators:

—died in Wentworth, OH

—a Wentworth resident

Marielle Soderson

Desperation:

—lived

The Regulators:

—died in Wentworth, OH

—a Wentworth resident

Melissa Sweetheart

Desperation:

—a doll

The Regulators:

—an imaginary friend

Allen Symes

Desperation:

—a Desperation Mining Corporation employee

The Regulators:

—a Deep Earth Mining Corporation employee

Tak

Desperation:

—the bad guy

—blasting freed for a few days in 1996

—must have a host

—any human could host; an animal could host

The Regulators:

—the bad guy

—1994 blasting freed for two years

—could survive outside its host

—fed off others' energy and lifeforces

—only special humans could host

Worrell

Desperation:

—Worrell's Market in modern-day Desperation, NV

The Regulators:

—Worrell's Mercantile in The Regulators, a Western

Audrey Wyler

Desperation:

—died in Desperation, NV

—single

The Regulators:
—lived
—a Wentworth, OH, resident

Appendix 7: Writers

Many Stephen King characters are writers of one sort or another.

Novelists and Bestselling Authors

Roberta Anderson *The Tommyknockers*
Westerns

Claudia y Inez Bachman *The Dark Tower*
Charlie the Choo-Choo!

Richard Bachman *The Dark Tower*
a Stephen King pseudonym

Olive Barker *The Plant*
the *Windhover* series

Thaddeus Beaumont *The Dark Half*
also wrote as George Stark

William Bunting *American Vampire*
Bad Blood or the Monster Outlaw: A Terrifying Tale of the Old West

Robert D. M. Cannon *The Shining* deleted scene
a bestselling author

Jinky Carstairs *The Plant*
paperback publisher: Zenith House

James Curran *The Plant*
paperback publisher: Zenith House

William Denbrough *IT*
wrote about Creatures from Beyond the Universe

Michael Enslin "1408"
Ten Nights in Ten Haunted ___ series

Beryl Evans *The Dark Tower*
Charlie the Choo-Choo!

Franklin Fay *Revival*
poetry

Gault "The Mist"
a paperback each year

David Goodis *Rose Madder*
Dark Passage (1946)

Stephanie Weider Gravel-Miller *Duma Key*
Boat Trips and Beeswax: A Girlhood in Nokomis, an ebook memoir on John Eastlake

Richard Hagstrom "The Word Processor"
short stories and articles

Nick Hardaway *The Plant*
the *Macho Man* series

Rick Hardin "Rest Stop"
a John Dykstra pseudonym

Tessa Jean "Big Driver"
The Willow Grove Knitting Society series

Peter Jeffries "Dedication"
World War I and World War II stories

Robert Jenkins "The Langoliers"
mysteries

Steve Kemp *Cujo*
Chasing Sundown, a book of poetry

Richard Kinnell "The Road Virus Heads North"
horror

Stephen King *The Dark Tower*

Gordon Lachance "The Body"

novels about people with Extra Sensory Perception

Scott Landon *Lisey's Story*
won a National Book Award and a Pulitzer Prize

Samuel Landry "Umney's Last Case"
a series about Private Investigator Clyde Umney

Drew Larson "Rat"
Bitter River, a Western

Anthony L.K. LaScorbia *The Plant*
the *Nasty Creatures from Hell* series

John Marinville *Desperation*
won a National Book Award

John Marinville *The Regulators*
Pat the Detective Kitty children's series

Stephen W. Meader *IT*
Bulldozer

Benjaman Mears *'Salem's Lot*
went to 'Salem's Lot to write his fourth book

Jamie Morton *Revival*
wrote about Charlie Jacobs, his fifth business

Gerald Nately "The Blue Air Compressor"
wrote four novels

Michael Noonan *Bag of Bones*
a bestselling novelist

Ollinger *The Dark Half*
science fiction

Paul "The Ballad of the Flexible Bullet"
his first novel sold well

Gwendy Peterson *Gwendy's Magic Feather*
Gwendy's Final Task
several novels and a non-fiction piece

Morton Rainey "Secret Window, Secret Garden"
plagiarized a short story before becoming a bestselling writer

Richard Rancine *Rose Madder*
a Christina Bell pseudonym

Cammie Reed *The Regulators*
a writer

Concetta Reynolds *Doctor Sleep*
twenty poetry books

Clayton Riddell *Cell*
Dark Wanderer graphic novels

Norbert Rosen "The Breathing Method"
Stedham & Son, New York and Boston, published three volumes of poetry.

Peter Rosewall "Dedication"
Blaze of Glory (1985)

John Rothstein *Finders Keepers*
The Jimmy Gold Trilogy

Edward Gray Seville "The Breathing Method"
Stedham & Son published at least eleven novels.

Paul Sheldon *Misery*
the *Misery* romance series

George Stark *The Dark Half*
a Thaddeus Beaumont pseudonym

Bart I. Straight *The Plant*
the Coldeye Denton westerns

Reg Thorpe "The Ballad of the Flexible Bullet"
novel: *Underworld Figures*
short story: "The Ballad of the Flexible Bullet"

William Weiderman "Sorry, Right Number"
horror

NON-FICTION WRITERS

Branson Buddinger *IT*
A History of Derry

David R. Congress *Carrie*
The Shadow Exploded: Documented Facts and Specific Conclusions Derived from the Case of Carietta White

John R. Coombs *Carrie*
Slang Terms Explained: A Parents' Guide

Susan Day *Insomnia*
Lilies of the Valley, about battered women, won a Pulitzer Prize

Janet Freestone-Love *The Plant*
Your New Astral Cookbook

Fricke *IT*
Old Derry-Town

M. K. Handey *IT*
Guide to North American Birds

Michaud *IT*
History of Derry

Susan Snell *Carrie*
My Name is Susan Snell

C. K. Summers "The Jaunt"
The Politics of the Jaunt

Magazine, Newspaper, and Tabloid Reporters

Josh Brannigar *The Shining*

David Bright *The Dead Zone*
The Tommyknockers
the Bangor *Daily News*

William Bunting *American Vampire*
wrote for Sensation Press

Ernie Calvert *11/22/63*
the Dallas *Morning News*

Hal Collier "After the Play"
The Denver Post

Rodney Conklin *The Shining*
a Financial Editor of a Denver newspaper

Craig "Mr. Harrigan's Phone"
the *Times-Union*

Richard Dees *The Dead Zone*
"The Night Flier"
Inside View

Mike Donaldson *The Dark Half*
People magazine

Mack Dugas *11/22/63*
the Dallas *Morning News*

Roger Dussault *The Dead Zone*
a Lewiston *Sun* feature editor

C. Anthony Eddington III *Lisey's Story*

the U-Tenn *Review*, the U-Tenn Nashville campus newspaper

David Felton *The Shining*
a Feature's Editor of a Denver newspaper

Fletcher "In the Deathroom"
The New York Times

Joseph Gargan *The Talisman*
The Angola Herald in Angola, NY

Burt Hammersmith "The Green Mile"
the Tefton *Intelligencer*

Hanratty *The Colorado Kid*
the Boston *Globe*

Eddie Hughes *11/22/63*
the Dallas *Morning News*

Devin Jones *Joyland*
Cleveland, *Commercial Flight*

John Leandro *The Tommyknockers*
the Bangor *Daily News*

Michael Leith *Misery*
the Denver *Post*

John Lewis *'Salem's Lot*
a Portland *Press-Herald* Features Editor

Max H. Littell *11/22/63*
the *Daily News*

Robert T. McCord "After the Play"
The Estes Park Echo

James T. Mears *Blaze*
the *Evening Express*

Betsy Moriarty "The Monkey"

The Bridgton News

M. Rickert *Duma Key*
the Port Charlotte *Weekly Echo*

Philip Scudder *11/22/63*
the *Daily News*

Julia Shumway *Under the Dome*
the Chester's Mill *Democrat*

James Whitney *The Plant*
The New York Times

Writers with Magazine and Book Appearances

Bourke and **Hannegan** *Carrie*
"A View Toward Isolation of the TK Gene with Specific Recommendations for Control Parameters"

Jack Gaver *Carrie*
"Carrie: The Black Dawn of TK" in *Esquire*

Professor George Jerome *Carrie*
The Atlantic Monthly

Sandy Ives *IT*
a series of articles about Derry, ME, history

John Kenton *The Plant*
stories in "sensitive" magazines

Lubert *'Salem's Lot*
an article about the Marstens

Dean D.L. McGuffin *Carrie*
"Telekinesis: Analysis and Aftermath"

Adrian Mellon *IT*

an article about Derry's Canal for *New England Byways* (in progress)

John P. Muller *The Regulators*
an article about the MotoKops in *Playthings, The International Merchandising Magazine of the Toy Industry*

Richard Price "The Library Policeman"
"THE JUNCTION CITY PUBLIC LIBRARY—One Hundred Years of History," appeared in a special library supplement to the Junction City *Gazette*.

Thomas Ross *Carrie*
a poem in *Everleaf*

Richard T. Rumsfeld *From a Buick 8*
"We Have Been Visited!" for *Inside View*

Snow *'Salem's Lot*
an article about the Marstens

Selena St. George *Dolores Claiborne*
various magazines, including *The Atlantic Monthly*

John Torrance *The Shining*
wrote short stories

Norma Watson *Carrie*
"We Survived the Black Prom," a *Reader's Digest* "Drama in Real Life" story

White and **Stearns** *Carrie*
"Telekinesis: A Wild Talent Revisited"

Freelance Writers

Howard Fornoy "The End of the Whole Mess"

James Gardener *The Tommyknockers*
a Full-Time Poet ("Leighton Street")

Myers *The Cannibals*

James Upshaw *The Cannibals*
wrote greeting-card verse

Mort Yeager *The Plant*
a ghost writer for Zenith House

Writers for Academia

Louis Creed *Pet Sematary*
The Magazine of College Medicine and others

Michael Cunningham *Christine*
a history professor at Horlicks University
specialty: military history

Peter Jackson *Desperation*
an assistant English professor at NYU
specialty: postwar American fiction

Peter Jackson *The Regulators*
an assistant English professor at Ohio State

Peter Mark Stein *Lisey's Story*
Cutting Behavior

Professor Joseph Woodbody *Lisey's Story*
articles about Scott Landon's work

Songwriters

Jory Baker *The Stand*
wrote for Sparx

W. Denbrough *Duma Key*
R. Tozier and W. Denbrough wrote the lyrics to "Dig," performed by Shark Puppy

Sara Tidwell *Bag of Bones*

wrote songs for Sara and the Red-Tops

R. Tozier *Duma Key*

R. Tozier and W. Denbrough wrote the lyrics to "Dig," performed by Shark Puppy

Richie "Records" Tozier *The Girl Who Loved Tom Gordon*

wrote the lyrics to "Gotta Get Next to You (Jus' Slip Me a Taste)," performed by Boyz To Da Maxx

Larry Underwood *The Stand*

wrote for the Tattered Remnants and his solo act
big hit: "Baby, Can You Dig Your Man?"

Screenwriters

William Denbrough *IT*

Pit of the Black Demon based on his novel *The Black Rapids*; *The Attic Room*

Craig Goodis *The Regulators*

He and Quentin Woolrich wrote *The Regulators*, a Western.

Michael Noonan *Bag of Bones*

The Red-Shirt Man, adapted from his novel of the same name

Quentin Woolrich *The Regulators*

He and Craig Goodis wrote *The Regulators*, a Western.

Unpublished Writers

George Amberson *11/22/63*

The Murder Place and his travels to the Land of Ago

Dr. John Bonsaint "N."

a case study on N.

Carlos Detweiller *The Plant*
True Tales of Demon Infestations

Paul Edgecombe "The Green Mile"
a manuscript on John Coffey and the Green Mile

Michael Hanlon *IT*
Derry: An Unauthorized Town History aka *Derry: A Look Through Hell's Back Door*

General Anthony Hecksler *The Plant*
Twenty Psychic Garden Flowers

Harold Lauder *The Stand*
strange short stories written with an unconventional style

Bob Polhurst *Insomnia*
Later That Summer about the aftermath of the Battle of Gettysburg

James Saltworthy *The Plant*
The Last Survivor

John Shooter "Secret Window, Secret Garden"
"Secret Window, Secret Garden"

Billy Summers w/**Alice Maxwell** *Billy Summers*
Billy Summers: The Story of a Lost Man

Riddley Walker *The Plant*
worked on a novel

Appendix 8: List of Works

<u>NOVELS:</u>

1974: *Carrie*
1975: *'Salem's Lot*
1977: *The Shining*
Rage
1978: *The Stand* (updated in 1990)
1979: *The Long Walk*
The Dead Zone
1980: *Firestarter*
1981: *Roadwork*
Cujo
1982: *The Running Man*
1982: *The Dark Tower I: The Gunslinger*
1983: *Christine*
Pet Sematary
1984: *The Talisman*
Thinner
1985: *Cycle of the Werewolf*
1986: *IT*
1987: *The Eyes of the Dragon* (revised from a previously released limited edition)
The Dark Tower II: The Drawing of the Three
Misery
The Tommyknockers
1989: *The Dark Half*
1991: *The Dark Tower III: The Waste Lands*
Needful Things
1992: *Gerald's Game*
Dolores Claiborne
1994: *Insomnia*

1995: *Rose Madder*
1996: *The Green Mile*
Desperation
The Regulators
1997: *The Dark Tower IV: Wizard & Glass*
1998: *Bag of Bones*
1999: *Storm of the Century*
The Girl Who Loved Tom Gordon
Hearts in Atlantis (a set of stories so closely related I'm including it with the novels)
2000: *The Plant*
2001: *Dreamcatcher*
Black House
2002: *From a Buick 8*
2003: *The Dark Tower V: Wolves of the Calla*
2004: *The Dark Tower VI: Song of Susannah*
The Dark Tower VII: The Dark Tower
2005: *The Colorado Kid*
2006: *Cell*
Lisey's Story
2007: *Blaze*
2008: *Duma Key*
2009: *Under the Dome*
2011: *American Vampire* (graphic novel)
11/22/63
2012: *The Dark Tower 4.5: The Wind Through the Keyhole*
2013: *Joyland*
Doctor Sleep
2014: *Mr. Mercedes*
Revival
2015: *Finders Keepers*
2016: *End of Watch*
2017: *Gwendy's Button Box*
Sleeping Beauties

2018: *The Outsider*
Elevation
2019: *The Institute*
Gwendy's Magic Feather
2021: *Later*
Billy Summers
2022: *Gwendy's Final Task*
Fairy Tale
TBD: *Holly*

NOVELLA COLLECTIONS:

1982: *Different Seasons*
1990: *Four Past Midnight*
2010: *Full Dark, No Stars*
2020: *If It Bleeds*

SHORT STORY COLLECTIONS:

1978: *Night Shift*
1985: *Skeleton Crew*
1993: *Nightmares & Dreamscapes*
2002: *Everything's Eventual*
2008: *Just After Sunset*
2015: *The Bazaar of Bad Dreams*

Books by Michael Roch

Bumpty-Bumpty-Bump!: The Stephen King Daily Reader

Fun is Fun and Done is Done: Stephen King Connections and Easter Eggs

Milton Keynes UK
Ingram Content Group UK Ltd.
UKHW021258090923
428369UK00021B/640

9 798986 152103